WOMEN *of* COURAGE

WOMEN *of*
COURAGE

a FORTY-DAY DEVOTIONAL

B&H
PUBLISHING
NASHVILLE, TENNESSEE

(in)courage editor **Mary Carver**

Published by B&H Publishing Group
Nashville, Tennessee

Dewey Decimal Classification: 248.843

Subject Heading: WOMEN / COURAGE / WOMEN IN THE BIBLE

Cover design by Emily Strnad. Cover photo © Rawpixel.com/shutterstock.
Cover illustration © Anugraha Design/Creative Market

Photography, shutterstock: pg 4 savageultralight; pg 8: Olha Afanasieva; pg
12: Claudia Knopf; pg 16:Viktor Gladkov; pg 26: antoniodiaz; pg 32: lily_of_
the_valley; pg 36: ptnphoto; pg 40: Andrei Mayatnik; pg 44: JFragments;
pg 48: Wichete Ketesuwan; pg 58: Aline Fortuna; pg 62: Dubova; pg 66:
Melanie Hobson; pg 70: Yulia Grigoryeva; pg 76: coka; 92: A. and I. Kruk; pg
98: Richard Lyons; pg 102: Brainsil; pg 106: WichitS; pg 114: Song_about_
summer; pg 120: aliasemma; pg 124: cdrin; pg 128: mama_mia; pg 132: Diana
Taliun; pg 136: Romas_Photo; pg 142: Rawpixel.com; pg 146: Alena Ozerova;
pg 152: eldar nurkovic; 156: Elly Photography; pg 160: Nevada31; 164: Bill45;
pg 178: Jit-anong Sae-ung

Photography, unsplash: pg 84: josh appel; pg 89: taylor ann wright; pg 110:
eye-for-ebony; pg 168: priscilla-du-pree; pg 174: omar-lopez

Photography, (in)courage: pg 54: Luke Davis, Main Street Studios, Siloam
Springs, AR

1 2 3 4 5 6 7 • 23 22 21 20 19

Contents

Introduction

Hello, **DEAR FRIEND! WE'RE SO** glad you've picked up this devotional. Created as a companion for the (in)courage Devotional Bible, this book features brave women of the Bible. Many of these women are featured in the devotional Bible, but here we dive deeper into their stories and their hearts, sharing the incredible inspiration we've found for facing our lives with courage.

After all, if you're like us, you're probably looking for a little courage—or a lot of courage. We know how overwhelming—and sometimes even scary—life can be. We know how it feels to enter a new opportunity, a difficult situation, or even just the "everydayness" of life and wonder . . .

How am I going to do this?

Am I strong enough?

Am I brave enough?

Am I the only one who's felt this anxious or scared?

Can anyone help me figure this out?

Can anyone show me how to find courage?

When we dive into the Bible for answers and inspiration, God provides deep meaning and real guidance for our lives through the stories of women in His Word. Though they lived hundreds of years ago, women from Sarah and Naomi to Lydia and the woman at the well can teach us so much about facing brokenness and hopelessness with courage today.

These are not the Sunday school lessons of your childhood! No catchy choruses or flannel-graph dolls here. When we decided to look to the women of the Bible to learn about living courageously, we opted out of the surface level stories and simple platitudes we've been given in the past. Instead, we took a more personal approach and got to know these ladies at a deeper, more meaningful, more relatable level.

Our hope is that by putting yourself in these women's sandals, you can walk the same brave roads they did, through brokenness, betrayal, and tragedy, to gratitude, hope, and second chances. We hope you can learn, just as we are, to live courageously despite unusual, difficult, or even frightening circumstances.

Featuring forty brave women—some well-known (like Ruth, Elizabeth, Mary, and Martha) and some lesser-known (such as Shiprah, Puah, Lois, and Eunice)—this devotional will walk with you through the hardest days and leave you with the courage you need to lead, to love, to trust, and to turn to God in every situation. From women who were called to step into leadership roles to women who had to rely on God's daily provision for their needs, these heroes of the Bible show you exactly how to lean into the strength of the Lord when your own isn't enough.

Each reading begins with a passage of Scripture, then delves into a woman's story with detail and depth that illustrates exactly how much she was loved and cared for by God. It ends with encouragement to apply the day's lesson in your own life and a personal prayer that gets right to the heart of the matter and more importantly, the heart of God Himself.

May each of us begin this journey with honesty and openness, prepared to be inspired and moved closer to the One who gives us strength and courage as we spend time with some incredible women of the Bible.

BECOME A WOMAN OF COURAGE! BE PART OF THE (IN)COURAGE COMMUNITY WITH DAILY DEVOTIONS DELIVERED STRAIGHT TO YOU. JOIN US AT WWW.INCOURAGE.ME.

WOMEN *of* BEAUTIFUL BROKENNESS

Naomi

Boaz took Ruth and she became his wife. He slept with her, and the LORD granted conception to her, and she gave birth to a son. The women said to Naomi, "Blessed be the LORD, who has not left you without a family redeemer today. May his name become well known in Israel. He will renew your life and sustain you in your old age. Indeed, your daughter-in-law, who loves you and is better to you than seven sons, has given birth to him." Naomi took the child, placed him on her lap, and became his nanny. The neighbor women said, "A son has been born to Naomi," and they named him Obed. He was the father of Jesse, the father of David.

(RUTH 4:13–17)

Naomi WAS NO STRANGER TO brokenness. Her life was marked by loss and difficulty. Her husband and two sons died at an early age, which in her culture at the time, meant that she had no provision, future, or safety. She also lived in a foreign land, which would have further isolated her from the tight-knit community around her. Her life was hard, and her heart was becoming hard as well. She even insisted on being called "Mara," which means "bitter," because she said, "[T]he Almighty has made me very bitter. I went away full, but the LORD has brought me back empty. Why do you call me Naomi, since the LORD has opposed me, and the Almighty has afflicted me?" (Ruth 1:20b–21).

Yet even in this state of devastation and grief, Naomi kept moving forward. Though she was convinced that God had turned His back on her, she returned to the land of promise anyway. While she initially tried her best to discourage her daughters-in-law from accompanying her on the journey, she eventually accepted Ruth's determination to go with her. As this faithful daughter-in-law stuck by Naomi's side and provided for the two of them, Ruth's friendship began to soften Naomi's heart to see the mighty work God was doing in both of their lives.

Naomi truly began to see the Lord's faithfulness to her and her family when Ruth providentially met Boaz, the one distant relative who was not only legally required to care for these women, but was also kind toward them. That glimmer of hope fed Naomi's faith, inspiring her to counsel Ruth toward the relationship with Boaz that God had prepared for her. By following her mother-in-law's advice, Ruth eventually married Boaz and gave Naomi a grandson. And not just anyone grandson, but one who would be part of the lineage of Jesus! What a gift of redemption!

Instead of turning his back on Naomi, God was stepping in right beside her through the friendship and loyalty of Ruth, the provision of Boaz, and eventually, the saving grace of Jesus Christ. Naomi's story may have journeyed through brokenness, but it doesn't end there.

Are you, like Naomi, bitter about your life? Are you convinced the Lord has taken everything from you and left you alone? Are you certain this is the end, the way it will always be?

Will you consider that perhaps your life is not over, that perhaps God still has plans for you—good plans to help you and not to harm you? Oh, friend, just look at what He did for Naomi! Look at the way He used Ruth to keep her from the deepest pit of despair, give her the tiniest bit of hope when things seemed most dire, and redeem her enormous loss for blessings beyond her imagination.

Your story is not finished yet. If heartache has found you and sent you spiraling into brokenness and darkness, hang on. God will not leave you in that place. He has not abandoned you, and He will not forget you. As you grieve and process, keep moving forward. When others reach out to you, let them in. And watch for signs of life in your battered heart. Hold onto any bit of hope you have with all your might and see how God will nurture it and multiply it. See how He will rescue you, care for you, and redeem every loss you've endured.

Remember that, though you may not see it now, God has a way of stepping right beside you in ways you wouldn't expect. In fact, He's already done more than simply stepped *beside* you. He has *taken your place*, bearing the worst of circumstances on your behalf through Christ's sacrifice on the cross. Remember that Jesus has endured the worst forms of pain and isolation, and He did it for you. Remember that whatever type of darkness you are facing, He understands.

> **HE'S ALREADY DONE MORE THAN SIMPLY STEPPED *BESIDE* YOU. HE HAS *TAKEN* YOUR PLACE.**

He's been there, and He can comfort you in it. What Naomi was looking forward to in her grandson's lineage is the very same Savior you look back on from your moment in history. Her hope is your hope, and that hope is Jesus Christ.

Though Naomi was bitter, afflicted, and empty for a while, she did not stay that way. Though she did not believe the Lord would change her situation, He did. And as she saw Him working in her life, Naomi chose to believe in the Lord's deliverance in the midst of her brokenness. God faithfully intervened and redeemed her story, giving her provision, security, and even allowing her to hold and care for her grandson. She saw God's faithfulness despite her brokenness, and saw the beauty that came from her suffering.

May our eyes be trained on God and His faithfulness even during our hardest seasons. May we remember that God has already entered in the middle of our brokenness through His Son—the One who stepped into our world and took on the worst for us. If He stepped into our brokenness then, He will certainly step into the places we need Him to now. As we trust this truth, like Naomi, we will be able to see the beauty He creates from the ashes of our suffering.

Prayer

God, this is hard. This is unbearably hard, harder than anything I've ever gone through. And I'm afraid my heart is just about as hard as my life right now. I feel so hopeless, so empty. I don't actually know if You can even hear me right now; it seems like You've left me to deal with everything all on my own. It feels like a punishment. It feels like the end, like things will never get better. I just don't know how to move on. Will You show me? Do You even still care? Will You help me get through this? Will there ever be a day when things don't seem so dark? Will I see Your light again? Will I smile again? Will I believe again?

Lord, I know that through Christ, You've already stepped into history to help me when I couldn't help myself. I know that, though I can't feel it, You promise that You are right beside me now, working all things together for my good and Your glory. I know You've done it before and, as the faith I used to feel so strongly would indicate, You'll do it again.

You've rescued and redeemed so many of Your children, like Naomi. So, God, I ask that You do it again, that You do it for me. Rescue me. Redeem my life and my story. Keep my heart from becoming as hard as my circumstances, and show me how You are working in my life to create something beautiful out of my brokenness. Thank You, God. For loving me and saving me and stepping into this pit with me instead of leaving me alone. I love You. Amen.

DAY 2

Woman with Jar of Perfume

And a woman in the town who was a sinner found out that Jesus was reclining at the table in the Pharisee's house. She brought an alabaster jar of perfume and stood behind him at his feet, weeping, and began to wash his feet with her tears. She wiped his feet with her hair, kissing them and anointing them with the perfume.

(LUKE 7:37–38)

Does **ANY OTHER PHYSICAL SIGN** show brokenness like weeping? The woman who anointed Jesus' feet with perfume in Luke 7 shows how beautiful our brokenness can be. She knew she was a sinner, and so did everyone else in the room. She was known for her sins all over town, making her a social outcast. But her brokenness didn't keep her from Jesus. She knew she would not be cast out with Him. She knew He was the One who would save her.

Desperate to show her gratitude, she brought an incredibly expensive bottle of perfume and anointed her Lord. The aroma no doubt filled the noses of everyone in the room while her weeping filled their ears. Her actions in this moment would have seemed improper to everyone watching, but she clearly did not mind. Unlike those around her, she understood the debt Jesus forgave, and this made her courageous in front of those who would usually make her hang her head in shame. She was no longer overcome with brokenness, but with gratitude. Her brokenness became beautiful when she encountered her Lord.

The Pharisee who was hosting Jesus for dinner that night did not see this brokenness and courage as a beautiful thing, however. He didn't immediately understand Jesus' response to this woman. *Doesn't Jesus know what a sinner she is?* he wondered. *How dare she carry on that way? How dare He let her do so? Given her reputation around town, doesn't He know what this looks like?*

Jesus answered with a parable of two forgiven debtors, one who owed much more than the other. His story made sense of why the woman was so emotional, and also why Jesus accepted her grand display of gratitude as a beautiful gift instead of a waste of money or an improper gesture.

Turning to the woman, he said to Simon, "Do you see this woman? I entered your house; you gave me no water for my feet, but she, with her tears, has washed my feet and wiped them with her hair. You gave me no kiss, but she hasn't stopped kissing my feet since I came in. You didn't anoint my head with olive oil, but she has anointed my feet with perfume. Therefore I tell you, her many sins have been forgiven; that's why she loved much. But the one who is forgiven little, loves little." Then he said to her, "Your sins are forgiven." (Luke 7:44–48)

The woman knew her sins well; she knew just how much mercy she'd been given. And she wanted to lavish that same amount of love back onto the One who'd freed her. But the Pharisee, unsure of Jesus' power and perhaps unwilling to admit the depth of his own sins, hadn't experienced that same grace and therefore could not comprehend offering adoration with such abandon. Jesus' take on things pinpointed the problem: the Pharisee couldn't express an overwhelming level of love because he had not experienced that level of forgiveness.

In our so-called polite society, emotional displays are often sneered at, judged as messy and unnecessary, or even offensive. That wide brush paints all sorts of behaviors as "too much," whether it comes in the form of hands raised too high during worship, off-key voices singing too loudly, a flood of tears pouring out during a sermon, or exclamations of "praise Jesus" in average conversations.

But why? Why do we value the reserved responses to Jesus, and ridicule the expressive ones? Is it only that the noisy, wet sounds of weeping offend our sense of modesty and propriety, or could it also be that it forces us to confront our own mess? That it brings us face to face with our own shame, our own hidden sin, removing our ability to pretend as if we're doing just fine by ourselves? Does encountering someone who radiates joy and praise make us uncomfortable because we secretly wish that were true of us? Does witnessing an overtly enthusiastic exchange of shame and guilt for mercy and grace make it clear that we are missing something? That perhaps we've gotten it all wrong?

When the Pharisee invited Jesus to his home, he probably expected to impress the teacher with a delicious dinner, beautiful presentation, or prominent dinner companions. He stood tall and proud, adopting the posture of judge and jury when the sinful woman dared to enter his home, kneel behind Jesus, and offer all she had. Instead, Jesus turned toward this woman, prostrate with her messy display of unfettered emotion, and raised her up as an example. He accepted her offering and assured her of His mercy and forgiveness.

Can you recall the last time you wept? Do you remember the circumstances that brought you to your knees either literally or figuratively? Did you feel relief as you let go of any pretense that you were okay, as you confessed with your tears that you needed comfort or forgiveness?

No matter what you are holding onto or hiding deep within your heart today, you are invited to bring it to Jesus. Our Savior will take it from you and turn everything hard and bitter and ugly into something lovely and beautiful and pleasing. We all want to display grand acts of trust, love, and worship to God. But what if it's not as hard as we think? What if it's simply showing up at His feet, offering your brokenness to Him, and allowing Him into your pain?

> TURN EVERYTHING HARD AND BITTER AND UGLY INTO SOMETHING LOVELY AND BEAUTIFUL AND PLEASING.

If you are burdened with brokenness today, come to Jesus. Like the woman in Luke 7, let Him see your regrets and your sorrow and your tears; then let Him wipe them away with great grace and forgiveness.

Prayer

Jesus, thank You for loving us before we ever loved You. Thank You for offering forgiveness to us in the moments when we stand stubborn and proud and also when we lie broken and ashamed. Lord, I ask that You reach past my reserve and shiny façade, into the regrets and scars I've been hiding and holding for so long in my heart. You know what lies beneath my composure and my pride. You know the doubt, fear, and shame that keep me from You. Forgive me, Lord, for the pain I've caused and the distance I've created between us. Please help me understand the debt You have paid on my behalf, and like the woman in Luke, help this translate into genuine and expressive worship for all You've done. I want to love much because I've been forgiven much, so take my burdens and secrets, and give me joy instead. Heal me. God, You are so merciful and amazing. I love You. Thank You, Jesus. Amen.

The Samaritan Woman

*A woman from Samaria came to draw water. Jesus said to her, "Give me a drink."
(For his disciples had gone away into the city to buy food.) The Samaritan
woman said to him, "How is it that you, a Jew, ask for a drink from me, a woman
of Samaria?" (For Jews have no dealings with Samaritans.) Jesus answered her,
"If you knew the gift of God, and who it is that is saying to you, 'Give me a drink,'
you would have asked him, and he would have given you living water." The woman
said to him, "Sir, you have nothing to draw water with, and the well is deep. Where
do you get that living water? Are you greater than our father Jacob? He gave us
the well and drank from it himself, as did his sons and his livestock." Jesus said
to her, "Everyone who drinks of this water will be thirsty again, but whoever
drinks of the water that I will give him will never be thirsty again. The water that
I will give him will become in him a spring of water welling up to eternal life." The
woman said to him, "Sir, give me this water, so that I will not be thirsty or have to
come here to draw water."*

*Jesus said to her, "Go, call your husband, and come here." The woman answered
him, "I have no husband." Jesus said to her, "You are right in saying, 'I have no
husband'; for you have had five husbands, and the one you now have is not your
husband. What you have said is true." The woman said to him, "Sir, I perceive
that you are a prophet. Our fathers worshiped on this mountain, but you say
that in Jerusalem is the place where people ought to worship." Jesus said to her,
"Woman, believe me, the hour is coming when neither on this mountain nor in
Jerusalem will you worship the Father. You worship what you do not know; we
worship what we know, for salvation is from the Jews. But the hour is coming, and
is now here, when the true worshipers will worship the Father in spirit and truth,
for the Father is seeking such people to worship him. God is spirit, and those who
worship him must worship in spirit and truth." The woman said to him, "I know
that Messiah is coming (he who is called Christ). When he comes, he will tell us all
things." Jesus said to her, "I who speak to you am he."*

(JOHN 4:7–26 ESV)

The SAMARITAN WOMAN WAS AT the right place at the right
time. This likely came as a surprise to her since she was drawing water in the
middle of the day rather than the more common morning hours, possibly to
avoid the townspeople who knew of her sins and were critical of her lifestyle.
Assuming no one else would want to face the heat, she probably walked to the
well in the hottest part of the day with hopes to be alone, to be left in peace.

But on this day her plans to keep to herself were thwarted by an unexpected Jewish man asking for a drink.

How startling and confusing and maybe even frustrating that encounter must have been at first! Not only was the well not deserted as she expected, but here was a man—a Jewish man—speaking to her—a Samaritan woman! Though she was acquainted with breaking the rules, she was likely surprised that a religious teacher would do so.

Perhaps the shock of the situation is what emboldened her to question Jesus outright, asking why He spoke to her and then where He got the mysterious living water He mentioned. Or perhaps she was simply moved that someone would speak to her kindly and openly. Maybe she thought she'd take advantage of a stranger's ignorance of her reputation and enjoy a conversation with someone who knew nothing of her past.

What the woman quickly realized, though, is that this was no stranger, and He somehow knew secrets about more than water. He knew *her*, past and all. Though she'd never met Jesus before that day, and He was presumably a visitor to her town, He knew exactly who she was and what she'd done. But what was equally baffling to this intimate knowledge was His response to it—and to her.

Even knowing what He did about her, Jesus still spoke to the woman at the well. He still asked her for water, then offered her living water. Though He named her sins and forced her to face the truth of her choices, He offered her mercy. He knew her—and He loved her anyway.

The woman at the well was broken, and that brokenness is what drew her to Jesus. He did not condemn her, but instead, revealed her sin for what it was and allowed her to see the truth. He showed her the difference between the life she had and the life she could have in Him. He changed all of her perceptions by breaking barriers and offering grace.

When Jesus gave the woman living water, she was no longer ashamed of her brokenness because He had provided a way out. The Samaritan woman walked to the well that day expecting to simply finish a repetitive, daily chore unnoticed. Yet that trip—and her encounter with Jesus—was far from mundane, and it changed her forever. Because she met the Savior who had seen and known her all along, she was transformed.

So changed was this woman that she couldn't contain her joy. She was no longer striving to remain hidden or unseen—in fact, instead of running *away* from the townspeople in shame, she ran *toward* them with good news. She led many in her town to Christ and many Samaritans believed because of her testimony. Her brokenness not only changed the course of her life and drew her to Jesus, but it also changed many lives in Samaria that day and in the days and weeks to come. That's beautiful brokenness.

Have you been avoiding your own brokenness? Looking the other way rather than facing the reality of choices you've made? Do you go out of your way to escape confrontation or conviction? Oh, friend, how weary you must be! How bruised and wary your heart must feel! How deeply you must long for rest, for compassion, for Living Water that washes clean and quenches thirst forever. The Samaritan woman reminds us of the good news—that because our sin has been dealt with, we don't ever have to hide. Not from Jesus. Not from the One who sees behind every mask we wear and knows intimately the truth of our hearts—and loves us anyway, calling us toward a changed life.

> BECAUSE OUR SIN HAS BEEN DEALT WITH, WE DON'T EVER HAVE TO HIDE. NOT FROM JESUS.

As we go about our everyday chores, our usual routines today, may we keep our eyes up and watching for Jesus. May we embrace an unexpected encounter with the One who quenches every thirst and washes away every sin. May we run toward those we usually shy away from, carrying good news of the God who knows them to the same level He knows us. May we accept His grace so fully that we let Him turn our brokenness to beauty.

Prayer

Jesus, I'm broken. I've made choices and taken roads that have led me to a lonely, hard place. And I'm tired of denying it. I'm tired of pretending I don't notice the looks or the whispers, especially when the condemnation comes from my own heart. Will You forgive me? Will You love me anyway? Lord, I know that You are the answer. I know that what You offer me freely is so much better than anything the world offers with a cost. I know You have already paid the price for my wandering, and I accept Your mercy. I need Your grace. Thank You, Jesus. Thank You for seeing me, knowing me, loving me, and changing me so I can be a bearer of Your gospel and grace to others. Amen.

Leah

Now Laban had two daughters: the older was named Leah, and the younger was named Rachel. Leah had tender eyes, but Rachel was shapely and beautiful. Jacob loved Rachel, so he answered Laban, "I'll work for you seven years for your younger daughter Rachel."

Laban replied, "Better that I give her to you than to some other man. Stay with me." So Jacob worked seven years for Rachel, and they seemed like only a few days to him because of his love for her.

Then Jacob said to Laban, "Since my time is complete, give me my wife, so I can sleep with her." So Laban invited all the men of the place and sponsored a feast. That evening, Laban took his daughter Leah and gave her to Jacob, and he slept with her. And Laban gave his slave Zilpah to his daughter Leah as her slave.

When morning came, there was Leah! So he said to Laban, "What is this you have done to me? Wasn't it for Rachel that I worked for you? Why have you deceived me?"

Laban answered, "It is not the custom in this place to give the younger daughter in marriage before the firstborn. Complete this week of wedding celebration, and we will also give you this younger one in return for working yet another seven years for me."

And Jacob did just that. He finished the week of celebration, and Laban gave him his daughter Rachel as his wife. And Laban gave his slave Bilhah to his daughter Rachel as her slave. Jacob slept with Rachel also, and indeed, he loved Rachel more than Leah. And he worked for Laban another seven years.

When the LORD saw that Leah was unloved, he opened her womb; but Rachel was unable to conceive. Leah conceived, gave birth to a son, and named him Reuben, for she said, "The LORD has seen my affliction; surely my husband will love me now."

She conceived again, gave birth to a son, and said, "The LORD heard that I am unloved and has given me this son also." So she named him Simeon.

She conceived again, gave birth to a son, and said, "At last, my husband will become attached to me because I have borne three sons for him." Therefore he was named Levi.

And she conceived again, gave birth to a son, and said, "This time I will praise the LORD." Therefore she named him Judah. Then Leah stopped having children.

(GENESIS 29:16–35)

Leah **WAS KNOWN FOR HER** "tender eyes," meaning that her eyesight may have been weak or that her eyes may have been crossed. She was given away in marriage, only to have her husband reject her the next morning, demanding he be given her younger "shapely and beautiful sister," Rachel.

While the culture of Leah's family is different than our own, we can surely imagine how she must have felt in this situation. Who isn't familiar with the soaring anticipation of a heart brave enough to hope, followed by the devastating crash when those hopes are ruined? Leah probably suspected her father's deception would anger Jacob, but after vows were spoken and embraces were exchanged, I wonder if she held a tiny bit of hope that Jacob would accept her after all.

Scripture doesn't downplay Jacob's response. He was outraged, demanding an explanation and dismissing Leah as someone unworthy of his attention or affection. How humiliating and heartbreaking this must have felt. However, even though Jacob wanted to move on to his preferred sister, Leah's story wasn't finished.

Leah was broken, no doubt. But the Lord saw Leah and how she was unloved, and He blessed her with children. At first, she mistakenly believed her children would bring her the love she was longing for from Jacob, her husband. She was wrong; however, with each child she bore, Leah grew closer and closer to her God. She learned to praise God in her brokenness and loneliness, giving joy to the One who always met her needs.

Leah's fourth son was named Judah, which sounds like "praise" in Hebrew. Judah led her to praise the Lord. Judah's descendants included some incredible men, like David, Solomon, and, eventually, Jesus. And it was Leah who was buried with the fathers of Israel in Abraham's tomb.

> **LEAH WAS UNLOVED AND BROKEN, BUT THE LORD TURNED HER BROKENNESS INTO PRAISE.**

Leah was unloved and broken, but the Lord turned her brokenness into praise, and ultimately, brought the Messiah into the world through her, and as we know, that Messiah would come to know what rejection and brokenness feels like. Like Leah, He would be unwanted, picked over, and disregarded by those He loved, too. More than that, He would die for the people who did those things to Him, and His weakness would not be seen merely on His face or in His eyes, but His entire body would break on the cross for all to see. Also like Leah, God would use His brokenness to bring many new "sons and daughters" into the family!

Are you feeling unloved today? Perhaps you've been overlooked, dismissed, or judged as someone not pretty enough, not smart enough, not organized or outgoing or creative enough. Perhaps you've been told you're not enough so many times that you finally believe it's true. Perhaps, like Leah, you are weak and broken.

If so, take heart in Leah's story! Look at how the Lord became enough for her when she thought "being enough" was all on her own shoulders. Look at the Savior who eventually came from her, the One who was rejected by others and broken for you, so that you could know and rest in God's comfort right now.

While the gift of children may not be the specific way God intervenes in your life, know that He will not forget you. Know that He will comfort you and bless you and walk beside you even when all others have abandoned you. He will be enough when you feel like you are not, and He will give you a reason to praise His name.

Lift your eyes to the One who is close to the brokenhearted, friend, for He knows how you feel. Lean on the One who longs to wipe away every tear. He will never reject you, never force you to earn His attention, never dismiss you for another. Run to the One whose own death turned into something beautiful, which means He has every power to turn *your* brokenness into something beautiful, healing your heart along the way.

Prayer

Heavenly Father, thank You for loving me better than anyone on earth can. Thank You for looking at my weak eyes and my bruised heart and calling me beautiful. It's hard to believe sometimes, though; help my unbelief. Heal the parts of me that feel unlovable and undeserving of Your blessings. Show me how to trust You, how to believe that You will never turn me away. Even when I feel overlooked and even when I am treated unfairly, God, I know that You are just and merciful and with me always. Thank You for facing the pain of being unwanted and unloved Yourself, so that You could understand how this feels. Thank You for being broken for me so that I could have life and mercy. Please flood me with Your presence in these painful times, and forgive any bitterness that has taken root. Thank You, Lord. I love You. Amen.

The Canaanite Woman

When Jesus left there, he withdrew to the area of Tyre and Sidon. Just then a Canaanite woman from that region came and kept crying out, "Have mercy on me, Lord, Son of David! My daughter is severely tormented by a demon."

Jesus did not say a word to her. His disciples approached him and urged him, "Send her away because she's crying out after us."

He replied, "I was sent only to the lost sheep of the house of Israel."

But she came, knelt before him, and said, "Lord, help me!"

He answered, "It isn't right to take the children's bread and throw it to the dogs."

"Yes, Lord," she said, "yet even the dogs eat the crumbs that fall from their masters' table."

Then Jesus replied to her, "Woman, your faith is great. Let it be done for you as you want." And from that moment her daughter was healed.

(MATTHEW 15:21–28)

The CANAANITE WOMAN WASN'T A Jew, yet she knew of the coming Messiah. She knew who Jesus was and knew what He could do. Her daughter was afflicted with a demon, one who tormented her day and night. Though she knew better than to approach a man like this so boldly, she did it anyway. With her daughter's life on the line, abiding by cultural norms wasn't an option for this mother. She simply did not have time to wait for Jesus to make His way to the Gentiles; she needed Him now.

Because she was not a Jew, the Canaanite woman was rejected and ignored. Jesus Himself tried to pass by her at first, staying on track with His mission of ministering to the lost sheep of Israel first. While the Gentiles were always part of God's plan of grace to save humanity, salvation was destined to start with the Jews and move outward from there, and Jesus was staying focused.

But this mother was desperate. Her brokenness led her to seek out the Healer. She had found Him and she was not going to stop asking or back down. If she had been proud, she might have taken offense at His refusal. She might have felt insulted that His response, on the surface, seemed so dismissive and unkind, as He referenced her people as "dogs," His people's common term for Gentiles. On the other hand, had her faith not been so strong, she may have let discouragement or disappointment stop her from continuing to ask for help. She might have thought Jesus wasn't the Savior she'd heard and believed He was.

But this mother was not only desperate to find help for her daughter; she was not only bold and determined to get the attention and mercy of the Messiah. No, she also was humbled to the point of brokenness, caring little what those watching thought of her urgent pleas for help. She had enormous, steadfast faith that was not shaken by silence or scolding or scorning. No hurdle was going to keep her from her Lord—or from the healing He could give her daughter.

> **NO HURDLE WAS GOING TO KEEP HER FROM HER LORD.**

Her persistence caused the Lord to speak to her. She understood great truths that even Jesus' disciples did not understand. She believed in who Jesus was and in His great power, despite His current calling to the Jews. Her brokenness gave way to great faith, and because of that great faith, Jesus commended her and healed her daughter. Her brokenness was made beautiful because of the incredible faith that resulted.

Are you carrying a burden today—grief or worry for a loved one, perhaps—that you are anxious to bring to the Lord? Are you desperate for a cure, a change, an answer, a redemption? Are you nervous that He may not hear you? That you might be ignored or turned away? Maybe you're nervous that your request is too small to bother Him with or too big to expect Him to help with. Perhaps you are afraid it's been too long since you talked to God, or perhaps you have even walked away from your faith for a while. Will He still hear you? Will He still answer?

Do you believe? Do you believe that God is who He says He is? That He's loving, merciful, and all-powerful? Then ask Him.

Are you humble? Are you laid bare on the floor, fully aware that nothing and no one else can help? Do you acknowledge that only God can change the circumstance breaking your heart? Then cry out to Him.

While you could shrink back, doubt, or be discouraged into silence, you can choose another way. Like the Canaanite woman, you can persist. Her faith was so strong and her pride so shattered that she immediately grasped something that others did not—something you can grasp, too. Jesus was not turning her away; He was simply testing her faith to allow her faith and humility to shine before granting her mercy and healing.

If you are in urgent, desperate need of healing or help in a certain area of your life, come to the Lord. He will hear you and, when you ask in faith and humility, He will answer you. The answer may be delayed or unexpected or wholly different than what you anticipated, but He will answer. With pure and humble hearts, let us draw near to Him with confidence, as we're urged in the book of Hebrews, so we can receive mercy, grace, and help in our time of need.

Prayer

Dear Jesus, help me! I am desperate, and I know You are mighty to save. I know You are the Son of God, the Messiah, the One who came to save us. I know You can do all things, and I know that You love me. I know You offer me Your love, though I did not earn it. Thank You, Jesus. Thank You for loving me, for saving me. Lord, I come to You today broken and battered and exhausted from carrying this burden. I come to You and lay this burden at Your feet, and I ask You to help. Please. Have mercy on me and help me the way I believe You—and only You—can. Thank You, Lord, for hearing my cries, seeing my faith, and answering my pleas. Thank You. Amen.

WOMEN
BETTER
TOGETHER

Shiphrah and Puah

A new king, who did not know about Joseph, came to power in Egypt. He said to his people, "Look, the Israelite people are more numerous and powerful than we are. Come, let's deal shrewdly with them; otherwise they will multiply further, and when war breaks out, they will join our enemies, fight against us, and leave the country."

So the Egyptians assigned taskmasters over the Israelites to oppress them with forced labor. They built Pithom and Rameses as supply cities for Pharaoh. But the more they oppressed them, the more they multiplied and spread so that the Egyptians came to dread the Israelites. They worked the Israelites ruthlessly and made their lives bitter with difficult labor in brick and mortar and in all kinds of fieldwork. They ruthlessly imposed all this work on them.

The king of Egypt said to the Hebrew midwives—the first whose name was Shiphrah and the second whose name was Puah—"When you help the Hebrew women give birth, observe them as they deliver. If the child is a son, kill him, but if it's a daughter, she may live." The midwives, however, feared God and did not do as the king of Egypt had told them; they let the boys live. So the king of Egypt summoned the midwives and asked them, "Why have you done this and let the boys live?"

The midwives said to Pharaoh, "The Hebrew women are not like the Egyptian women, for they are vigorous and give birth before the midwife can get to them."

So God was good to the midwives, and the people multiplied and became very numerous. Since the midwives feared God, he gave them families. Pharaoh then commanded all his people: "You must throw every son born to the Hebrews into the Nile, but let every daughter live."

(EXODUS 1:8–22)

Do **YOU KNOW THE STORY** of Shiphrah and Puah? Though they may not show up on flannel graphs or in VBS songs, these two women had an incredible calling. They were Hebrew midwives, commanded by the evil king of Egypt to kill all of the Hebrew baby boys as soon as they were delivered. But because these women feared God and were certain He had set aside the Israelites for His greater purposes, they listened to the King of the Universe instead of the King of Egypt. Instead of killing the Hebrew children, Shiphrah and Puah saved them.

What courage! Their choice was not just dangerous, but life-threatening. Shiphrah and Puah risked their own safety to ensure the safety of the Hebrew baby boys. They were willing to lay down their own lives so that others could live—a subtle foreshadowing of the coming Christ, who truly did lay down His life so that many who were headed toward death could live instead.

Shiphrah and Puah's belief in their God and their mission—and the support they received from one another—gave them strength. These women were stronger together, knowing that they could support each other in their task of saving the Hebrew boys. Together, they honored the Lord by their regard for human life. Together, they saved a generation of Israelites and gave hope to a frightened, oppressed people.

> **THESE WOMEN WERE STRONGER TOGETHER, KNOWING THAT THEY COULD SUPPORT EACH OTHER IN THEIR TASK.**

Women were not highly valued and had little to no rights during this time of history. Though everyone was required to obey the king's command, and Pharaoh certainly could have commanded his soldiers to do his bidding, it's possible that Pharaoh assumed that the midwives would be even more compliant than the average person due to both their gender and their profession. Since they were the ones delivering the babies, and were part of the Hebrew community themselves, they had immediate access to male infants in a way that the Egyptians didn't.

Whether it was due to their gender, their ethnicity, or their profession, Pharaoh singled them out to do the worst task imaginable for someone who has dedicated their life to bring a baby into the world. They were required to obey from a legal standpoint. But what he asked of them was so barbaric, so horrible that they simply could not obey. They knew that this order was contrary to God's laws and His love for human life. Their devout faith kept them from blindly following their king, and their actions revealed that ultimately, they revered their heavenly King more than their earthly one.

Still, how frightened the women must have been to blatantly ignore Pharaoh's command! Fortunately—or, rather, providentially—neither woman had to stand alone. She had her sister in faith standing beside her—someone to pray with, someone to serve with, and someone to stand firm with when the angry king demanded answers.

Throughout Scripture we are urged to live in community with other believers. Though we are weak and susceptible to temptation on our own, we are stronger when we have sisters beside us. Together, women are better—better able to serve the Lord, better able to stand against the enemy, better able to love their neighbors and fulfill their callings. Just as God said in the very beginning that it is not good for man to be alone, the same is true for us today. Alone we may find it too difficult to love our neighbor and serve our community, to keep moving forward when faced with challenges, and to stand up to evil when it attacks. But together, we can.

Are you facing a trial today? Are you being asked or tempted to follow the world's ways instead of God's? Are you weary in the work that you've been called to do? Then this is the perfect time to reach out to another believer. Connect with a sister in Christ. Pray with a friend; pray for a friend. Lean on those trusted few in your circle and draw strength from their faith.

If you don't have a Shiphrah or a Puah in your life, ask God for one. Ask God for someone to walk beside you as you follow His plans and complete His mission. Petition Him for a sister who will push you to revere God above everything else, who will help you lay down your life for the sake of others, like Shiphrah and Puah did for the Hebrew boys, and ultimately like Christ did for you. And believe with confidence that the Lord will provide you with exactly what—and who—you need.

Prayer

Heavenly Father, thank You for the example of these brave women. Even though we read about them just once, we know they were important not just for what they did, but how they did it. Thank You for teaching us that we are better together. God, I ask that You give me a Shiphrah or a Puah, that You send me a sister to lean on, to walk with, to serve with, to love. Please give me wisdom to discern who I can trust with my fears and struggles and to know who will stand with me as we follow Your calling. Thank You for preparing me for the mission You've created for me, and please send a sister into my life who will help me revere You above everything else, and lay down my life for others like Jesus has done for me. Give me strength to follow You. Amen.

WOMEN *of*
DAILY GRACE

Widow of Nain

Afterward he was on his way to a town called Nain. His disciples and a large crowd were traveling with him. Just as he neared the gate of the town, a dead man was being carried out. He was his mother's only son, and she was a widow. A large crowd from the city was also with her. When the Lord saw her, he had compassion on her and said, "Don't weep." Then he came up and touched the open coffin, and the pallbearers stopped. And he said, "Young man, I tell you, get up!"

The dead man sat up and began to speak, and Jesus gave him to his mother. Then fear came over everyone, and they glorified God," saying, "A great prophet has risen among us," and "God has visited his people. This report about him went throughout Judea and all the vicinity.

Then John's disciples told him about all these things. So John summoned two of his disciples and sent them to the Lord, asking, "Are you the one who is to come, or should we expect someone else?"

When the men reached him, they said, "John the Baptist sent us to ask you, 'Are you the one who is to come, or should we expect someone else?'"

At that time Jesus healed many people of diseases, afflictions, and evil spirits, and he granted sight to many blind people. He replied to them, "Go and report to John what you have seen and heard: The blind receive their sight, the lame walk, those with leprosy are cleansed, the deaf hear, the dead are raised, and the poor are told the good news, and blessed is the one who isn't offended by me."

(LUKE 7:11–23)

Jesus SPENT THE YEARS OF His ministry traveling. During that time He was often surrounded by crowds or, at the very least, His group of disciples that traveled with Him. Yet His compassion was so great that He could not ignore those suffering in His presence, whether they were close enough to grab His clothes or simply passing by on their own journeys.

On this day, Jesus met a woman grieving the loss of her son, and though a stop was probably not on the disciples' agenda (travel straight to Nain—check!), He was compelled to stop and help.

Familiar with the culture, Jesus didn't need to be told that this woman's grief was twofold. Not only was she mourning the loss of her son, but as a widow she was uncertain of her future as well. First her husband had died, and now her young son was also dead. She had no man to provide for her in a culture where women were dependent on the men in their families. She was likely exhausted and afraid. She was alone, with no hope of provision or help.

But Jesus saw her and He had compassion on her. He knew exactly where she was and what her circumstances were. He granted her the exact amount of grace she needed. For her, that day, it was bringing her son back from the dead.

The unnamed widow from the town of Nain received an incredible gift from Jesus. Though the woman certainly could not have expected such a miracle and Jesus certainly did not have to provide for her in such an extravagant manner, He knew that bringing the widow's son back to life would have far-reaching effects.

When it happened, we're told that those around her were overcome with fear and they glorified God. This miracle not only affected the widow, but also all of those around her. In this moment, Jesus was using a resurrection to point to something that was coming that was even greater than the miracle at hand. He was giving the people of Nain a picture of when *He* would come back from the dead. His resurrection, like this son's, would have far-reaching effects, too. It would not just affect Him, but anyone who might believe in Him. Just as the widow's story radiated beyond her, bringing many to faith, Jesus' resurrection would do the same. In so many ways, her local story was a glimpse of the global one that was to come.

God's grace never only affects one person, but it always extends in more ways than anyone can see. We can see this in the widow's story and also in Jesus' own resurrection story. God always grants grace in our circumstances, though the way in which He does this is unpredictable. Regardless of how He pours out His grace, we can rest assured that He always will.

Are you grieving a loss today? Reeling from a blow that seems insurmountable, a circumstance that's brought you to your knees? Are you uncertain about your future, unsure how your needs could possibly be met? Hold onto hope, friend! Though you may not see Him through your pain or your surroundings, Jesus is just around the corner.

We know God is near to the brokenhearted, and just like Jesus couldn't ignore the widow's tears, He will not ignore yours. That problem you can't believe could be solved, that ache that never seems to go away, that loss that has left you empty and cold—none of it is more powerful than Christ.

The widow from Nain didn't know that Jesus would be coming into her town right as she walked out. Likewise, the disciples and others traveling with Him probably didn't know a funeral procession would disrupt their day. But Jesus knew. He knew exactly when He would encounter her, and He knew that—just as desperately as the widow wanted her son back—He would desperately want to help her and, in doing so, spread the word of who He was.

> JUST LIKE JESUS COULDN'T IGNORE THE WIDOW'S TEARS, HE WILL NOT IGNORE YOURS.

In the same way, God knows your sadness. He knows where you are and the exact moment your path will intersect with His. He is mindful of your pain and compassionate toward you. He may relieve your burden altogether, or He may simply walk by your side and carry it with you for a time. However He chooses to help you, you can be sure He will provide you with everything you need at the exact right time. And when He does, those who witness it will be amazed by God's goodness and grace.

Prayer

God, thank You for being near when I am sad and scared. I need Your compassion so much; I need it today. This loss feels like it might be the end of me, and the future feels terrifying. I don't know why this has happened, and I don't know what will happen next. Please help me. Please provide for me. And God, I pray that what I'm facing right now would be just one part of the story You're writing in my life, that it would be one more way my life shines light on Your grace. Breathe new life into this circumstance that feels so dead, and use it to bring many to faith as You did with the widow and with Jesus. Thank You, Lord, for meeting me in my pain and drawing close when I am brokenhearted. Thank You for giving me exactly what I need when I need it. I love You. Amen.

Persistent Widow

Now he told them a parable on the need for them to pray always and not give up. "There was a judge in a certain town who didn't fear God or respect people. And a widow in that town kept coming to him, saying, 'Give me justice against my adversary.'

"For a while he was unwilling, but later he said to himself, 'Even though I don't fear God or respect people, yet because this widow keeps pestering me, I will give her justice, so that she doesn't wear me out by her persistent coming.'"

Then the Lord said, "Listen to what the unjust judge says. Will not God grant justice to his elect who cry out to him day and night? Will he delay helping them? I tell you that he will swiftly grant them justice. Nevertheless, when the Son of Man comes, will he find faith on earth?"

(LUKE 18:1–8)

Jesus WAS NOTORIOUS FOR USING parables to teach His followers. Sometimes the takeaway was crystal clear; other times, it was hard to discern and people left confused. In this case Jesus made the lesson easy to understand: Just like the Persistent Widow never stopped asking the judge for what she needed, we should never stop asking God for what we need.

The Persistent Widow was just that: persistent. She knew what she needed and was not afraid to ask for it, over and over and over. She sought justice from a crooked judge who did not fear God. Because of the woman's persistence, the judge granted her request. He was tired of being bothered and so he gave her what she wanted. Likewise, God responds to His people when they continually seek Him. He does not answer His people because He is annoyed, like the judge, but because He loves and cares for them and has their best in mind.

At another time Jesus told a series of parables that illustrated how, if even a fallible man will give good gifts, our loving, almighty God will give exponentially better gifts. In the same way the story of the Persistent Widow shows us just how vital it is that we make sincere prayer a habit. While the judge was a stranger, and one who had no interest in helping the widow, God is the closest friend we could have, and one who loves us, longs for relationship with us, and feels deep compassion for us in our times of need. And though the judge could only be approached at certain times and gave the widow no encouragement to keep presenting her case, Jesus' work on the cross has granted us complete access to His throne at any time, reminding us throughout Scripture to bring our needs and burdens and worries to Him.

So, if the corrupt and careless judge finally gave into the Persistent Widow, how much more can we expect God to listen to our requests and respond with grace? Jesus has done everything necessary to relieve our debt with the Judge of heaven, and more than that, make us the Judge's *children*. While the Persistent Widow had the right to petition the judge as a citizen, we have the right to ask God for whatever we need as His *kids*!

> **WE SHOULD NEVER STOP ASKING GOD FOR WHAT WE NEED.**

The Persistent Widow is an example of how God grants His people exactly what they need when they need it. He provides grace for His people each and every day, in the exact portions they require. The Persistent Widow continued to make her request of the one person who could give her what she needed. God is the true, faithful judge and father who grants His people help and grace when they ask for it.

Do you struggle to pray without ceasing? Are you discouraged from a season of prayers without answers? Are you beginning to wonder if God is even listening, or if He even cares? Don't give up! Over and over we are told in Scripture to bring our every care to Him, that He is concerned about the things that concern us, that He hears us and will answer our requests. No, the answer may not come right away. No, the answer may not be what we expect. But at just the right time, God's grace will be exactly what we need. The Judge and Father of heaven is on our side, and He delights in our asking.

We can so easily be discouraged, and just as easily we can be distracted. What is keeping you from crying out to the Lord day and night? Is it fear that your requests will be ignored? Or that what is breaking your heart or keeping you awake won't be important to the Lord? Don't be afraid! Don't ever be afraid to approach God with your open heart. He went through a great deal of pain and loss to give you this very right, and He wants you to exercise that right.

Trust that God loves you. He loves you and wants to hear from you. And He wants the opportunity to lavish you with grace and help, to answer your every request and meet your every need. He's waiting for you to ask.

Let us not grow weary of believing in God's goodness, in His desire to hear our requests. Let us come to Him boldly, sincerely, and constantly with endurance and faith that He will receive us and respond to those requests. Let us be like the Persistent Widow; let us pray and pray again. Let us never stop seeking the Lord.

Prayer

Dear God, how do You do it? How do You listen to me pray about the same things over and over—and still want to hear more? I don't understand it, but I'm so grateful for it. Please help me trust You. Help me believe that You love me enough to listen to me cry day and night, that You will give me the exact answer I need at the exact moment I need it most, that You will offer me grace upon grace if only I will keep turning to You. Thank You, Jesus, for giving me access to the Father who wants to hear my needs. Thank You for making His throne room approachable to me, and giving me a relationship with a God who is encouraging, just and merciful, generous and compassionate. Thank You for loving me. I love You, too. Amen.

Bathsheba

Then Nathan said to Bathsheba, Solomon's mother, "Have you not heard that Adonijah son of Haggith has become king and our lord David does not know it? Now please come and let me advise you. Save your life and the life of your son Solomon. Go, approach King David and say to him, 'My lord the king, did you not swear to your servant: Your son Solomon is to become king after me, and he is the one who is to sit on my throne? So why has Adonijah become king?' At that moment, while you are still there speaking with the king, I'll come in after you and confirm your words."

So Bathsheba went to the king in his bedroom. Since the king was very old, Abishag the Shunammite was attending to him. Bathsheba knelt low and paid homage to the king, and he asked, "What do you want?"

(1 KINGS 1:11–16)

Bathsheba **WAS A NOTORIOUS PART** of King David's most shameful season. Whether or not she willingly chose to commit adultery with the king is not known, but one thing is for sure: she was sought out by the king, and then lost her husband to David's scheme to cover up his own sin. Yet despite the turmoil that her relationship with David caused the royal household, Nathan showed Bathsheba great kindness. Recognizing Adonijah's attempt to steal the throne from Bathsheba's son, Solomon, Nathan advised her to approach King David and ask for confirmation that her son would not be supplanted as the next king.

Though Bathsheba had experienced heartache at the hand of David (her first husband, Uriah, was murdered, and her first child with the king died very young), she had no other choice but to approach him for the sake of her son's safety and future. So she wisely approached him with great courage, asking for what had been promised to her son by God Himself (1 Chron. 22:9–10). She explained what was happening outside the palace walls and reminded David that without his intervention, someone else would become king upon his death while Bathsheba and Solomon would be "regarded as criminals" (1 Kings 1:17–21). Nathan then showed her further kindness by confirming her words and encouraging the king to take action.

King David responded by saying, "Call in Bathsheba for me." So she came into the king's presence and stood before him. The king swore an oath and said, "As the LORD lives, who has redeemed my life from every difficulty, just as I swore to you by the LORD God of Israel: Your son Solomon is to become king after me, and he is the one who is to sit on my throne in my place, that is exactly what I will do this very day."

Bathsheba knelt low with her face to the ground, paying homage to the king, and said, "May my lord King David live forever!"

King David then said, "Call in the priest Zadok, the prophet Nathan, and Benaiah son of Jehoiada for me." So they came into the king's presence. The king said to them, "Take my servants with you, have my son Solomon ride on my own mule, and take him down to Gihon. There, the priest Zadok and the prophet Nathan are to anoint him as king over Israel. You are to blow the ram's horn and say, 'Long live King Solomon!'" (1 Kings 1:28–34)

Thanks to Nathan's kindness and foresight, as well as Bathsheba's courage and humility, David's final command was that Bathsheba's son Solomon would take the throne after him. Despite the difficult circumstances surrounding Bathsheba becoming David's wife, God showed favor to her, and His grace poured out on her life. Her son Solomon became a great king in Israel, just as God promised, building the temple of the Lord and administering a time of peace in Israel.

We never know when God is going to pour out His grace on our lives. Are you in a season of hardship or uncertainty? Are you uncertain how God will resolve the complicated situation you're facing? Don't despair and don't give up! He is moving right now, though you may not see it, connecting dots and pulling pieces of the puzzle together. Soon His grace will be so clear, so evident as He shows you how to handle your circumstances. In Bathsheba's case, Nathan was the way God intervened. In your story, it may be through a person or some other way, but know that His mercy and goodness will remove obstacles, heal pain, and make way for something new.

And when that day comes—when you see how God has been working on your behalf the whole time, how He's been guiding you and others toward the plans He had in store all along—don't forget Him. He remembered you, so remember Him. Fall on your knees to thank Him; give Him all the praise and honor and glory. His grace is offered so freely. May our gratitude flow just as freely!

> GOD REMEMBERED YOU, SO REMEMBER HIM.

Bathsheba was overwhelmed with gratitude and the grace that the Lord showed both herself and her son through Nathan's intervention and David's decision to honor God's instructions. Her prostrate response is an example of how to respond to God's grace. May we all have the very same response when we see God's hand at work in our own circumstances.

Prayer

Dear God, thank You for remembering me. Thank You for showing me grace, for giving me new mercies every day. Help me keep my eyes trained on You and wide open to see every good gift You give me. Lord, I need help right now. I'm not sure how to fix this situation, and I'm scared. Will You help me? I know I played a part in this mess; I know I'm partly to blame. Please forgive me, God. Forgive me and rescue me. I can't fix it on my own! I trust You, Lord, and I believe that You are already working on my behalf, that You will keep me safe and provide for my needs. Like You did with Bathsheba, I believe that You'll keep Your promises to me and provide for me when I'm scared. Please give me the courage You gave her, and help me trust You more. I'm so grateful for everything You have done for me and everything You will do. I need You, Lord. And I love You. Thank You. Amen.

Rahab

Before the men fell asleep, [Rahab] went up on the roof and said to them, "I know that the LORD has given you this land and that the terror of you has fallen on us, and everyone who lives in the land is panicking because of you. For we have heard how the LORD dried up the water of the Red Sea before you when you came out of Egypt, and what you did to Sihon and Og, the two Amorite kings you completely destroyed across the Jordan. When we heard this, we lost heart, and everyone's courage failed because of you, for the LORD your God is God in heaven above and on earth below. Now please swear to me by the LORD that you will also show kindness to my father's family, because I showed kindness to you. Give me a sure sign that you will spare the lives of my father, mother, brothers, sisters, and all who belong to them, and save us from death."

The men answered her, "We will give our lives for yours. If you don't report our mission, we will show kindness and faithfulness to you when the LORD gives us the land."

(JOSHUA 2:8–14)

All **BUT ONE MENTION OF** Rahab's name in Scripture includes the title "the prostitute." What a way to be remembered! However, the mention of Rahab's former way of life is not used as a judgment of her character, but rather a reminder of the way God redeemed her life. She'd been living a life of desperation and sin, but she'd also heard about a powerful God leading the Israelites through the desert—and she wanted to know more. Though she was from a pagan, Canaanite city, she feared God when she heard of all of the miracles He performed for His people in the wilderness. When God's people needed an ally, He was able to use Rahab and grow her faith.

The repeated mentions of Rahab's profession also illustrate something powerful—that God doesn't require perfection, only repentance. After all, if He had to wait for perfect people to carry out His good plans, He'd wait forever! No, God works in many mysterious ways, including the way He moves in and through the lives of sinners. When God's people asked for her help, Rahab didn't hesitate. She helped them, she protected them, and she kept her promises to them. In return, she was protected by them as well.

By faith Rahab the prostitute welcomed the spies in peace and didn't perish with those who disobeyed. (Heb. 11:31)

Rahab's obedience and faith were so noteworthy that she is mentioned in the Bible's "Hall of Faith," the eleventh chapter of Hebrews. Listed right alongside Noah, Abraham, Joseph, and Moses, Rahab is remembered for her service to the Lord and her faith in His good plans. And not only was her life (and the lives of her family members) spared when the Israelites took Jericho, she went on to play a significant role in what would become Jesus' family tree. She became the grandmother of Boaz (the husband of Ruth), and she was a direct descendant of King David. She is one of four women mentioned in the lineage of Christ.

Do you wear labels of your past sins? Do you identify as your former self, despite being a new creation in Christ? If you believe that Jesus has already paid the penalty for your sins and have asked forgiveness for your past, it is time to let go of those old wounds. You have a new identity in Christ and it is one who is forgiven! Who is beloved! Who is cherished and valued and a vital member of God's kingdom! You are not who you once were. You are not what you once did. You are clean and brand-new and exactly who God created you to be, and He wants to use you just like He wanted to use Rahab.

YOU ARE NOT WHAT YOU ONCE DID.

And remember—while you may grieve the choices you made in the past, you should not doubt God's ability to use every single part of your life—good, bad, and ugly—to reveal His glory. You may regret, but God always redeems.

Others identified Rahab by her former self; perhaps she even identified herself that way. But God honored her life and faith, showing her immense grace despite her past and her heritage. He took her in as one of His own people. His grace redeemed her life and changed her future.

As you reflect on your past, may you never question God's decision to adopt you into His family through Christ's work on the cross. May you accept His forgiveness and your new identity as a beloved child of God. May you take courage in the truth that Jesus has given you His record, and you no longer stand on your own. May you see clearly the ways God is working everything— the old and the new, the stained and the cleansed, the regret and the redemption—together for your good and His glory. May you be remembered for your faith and for the grace God gave you.

Prayer

Dear God, how can You love me? I know You say You forgive me, but the things I've done are so ugly. It's hard to believe You look at me and see anything other than my past. But I believe. I believe what I've heard and what I've seen—that Your Son took on the penalty for my past so I wouldn't have to, and offered me Your perfect record in return. I believe that You are all-powerful and all-loving. And I believe You are going to take every part of my life and use it for something beautiful. God, please forgive me—for my sins, for my doubt, for my fear. I thank You for what You've already done in my life, for the new life and new purpose You've given me. Go with me, God. Give me courage and faith to follow You even when I cannot see You. I love You. Amen.

Daughters of Zelophehad

The daughters of Zelophehad approached; Zelophehad was the son of Hepher, son of Gilead, son of Machir, son of Manasseh from the clans of Manasseh, the son of Joseph. These were the names of his daughters: Mahlah, Noah, Hoglah, Milcah, and Tirzah. They stood before Moses, the priest Eleazar, the leaders, and the entire community at the entrance to the tent of meeting and said, "Our father died in the wilderness, but he was not among Korah's followers, who gathered together against the Lord. Instead, he died because of his own sin, and he had no sons. Why should the name of our father be taken away from his clan? Since he had no son, give us property among our father's brothers."

Moses brought their case before the LORD, and the LORD answered him, "What Zelophehad's daughters say is correct. You are to give them hereditary property among their father's brothers and transfer their father's inheritance to them. Tell the Israelites: When a man dies without having a son, transfer his inheritance to his daughter. If he has no daughter, give his inheritance to his brothers. If he has no brothers, give his inheritance to his father's brothers. If his father has no brothers, give his inheritance to the nearest relative of his clan, and he will take possession of it. This is to be a statutory ordinance for the Israelites as the LORD commanded Moses."

(NUMBERS 27:1–11)

Mahlah, NOAH, HOGLAH, MILCAH, AND Tirzah were the daughters of a man named Zelophehad. Zelophehad died in the wilderness and left only his five daughters, no sons. In Israel, only sons could receive an inheritance from their fathers, so the sisters knew they were about to find themselves in a bad situation. And not only would they be left without anything to their names, their father's name—and his family's claim to any property— would end with him as well.

This experience was unfortunately common for women during the time of Moses. No one would assume Zelophehad's daughters were being punished by their community—their lot was the same as any woman's in their culture, and their fate was in line with the law at the time. But that doesn't mean the law couldn't be changed.

Given their actions, we can assume that Zelophehad raised his daughters to be wise, hardworking, and knowledgeable. However, their place and time in history placed a lot of limitations on their choices and behavior. To approach their leader and their community so boldly was a risk. We can only imagine how much courage they had to muster, how many pep talks they had to give each other, how much the battle between fear and determination wreaked havoc in their hearts.

Though they may have felt the urge to shrink back, fear—whether of punishment or humiliation—did not stop these women. They came before Moses, stated their case, and asked for an inheritance. They pointed out that their father had not died because of wrongdoing, that he did not deserve for his family name to die out simply because he had no sons. Then they bravely asked to inherit his property.

What they asked was no small request. What they asked was an amendment to the law—a request big enough that Moses consulted directly with God before answering them. To these courageous women who asked for an inheritance to keep their father's name alive, the Lord showed incredible grace. He granted their request, therefore changing the law in Israel. Moses declared for the first time in Israelite history that if a man did not have any sons to receive his inheritance, his inheritance would go to his daughters.

This decision was prompted by the brave daughters of Zelophehad, but it resulted in a blessing for *all* women of Israel. Because these sisters banded together to ask Moses for their inheritance, taking strength from each other and their belief in their family's name and God's promised land, the entire sisterhood of Israelites would benefit. God's grace is like that. Grace—as well as courage and obedience—often overflow from one life into the lives of others. These Israelite daughters teach us so much about this principle, but we also see it in the life of Christ, who gave all believers—sons *and* daughters—an eternal inheritance from the Father.

> **WHEN YOU STAND IN COMMUNITY, ASKING GOD TOGETHER FOR HIS PROVISION, HE WILL ANSWER YOU.**

Do you find yourself in a sticky situation today? Does your fate seem to be held in someone else's hands? Are you enduring unfair treatment that affects many people, not just you? Join forces with the women around you. Bring together your fellow sisters, pool your resources and confidence and strength, and use your combined power for good. Scripture tells us that we should encourage one another, and remind each other that God is with us. And we're told that when we approach the throne of God, He will hear us. So gather. And then approach Him with your request.

God's grace is overflowing and never-ending, and is often too much to be contained by one life. When you stand in community, asking God together for His provision, He will answer you. He always extends grace to His people, no matter their need, and He will usually do it in a way that not only impacts you, but blesses so many that come after you.

Prayer

Dear God, I need Your help, and I know I'm not the only one. Please give me courage to talk to my sisters, to the other women in this situation. Please send me to the ones who will lock arms with me and help me find the words to say. And be with us, Lord, when we ask for change. Give us boldness and confidence; give us wisdom and clarity for what to request. God, what's happening isn't fair, but it's always been this way. I don't see how it could ever change. But You know. You know how, because You are the way and the answer. You're the God who changes things. Thank You, Lord, for knowing exactly what we need and what will happen. Thank You for guiding us and giving us strength, and giving us an eternal inheritance in Your name that cannot be taken away, no matter what happens. Thank You for caring about each one of us. Thank You. I love You. Amen.

WOMEN *of* LEADERSHIP

Priscilla

After this, [Paul] left Athens and went to Corinth, where he found a Jew named Aquila, a native of Pontus, who had recently come from Italy with his wife Priscilla because Claudius had ordered all the Jews to leave Rome. Paul came to them, and since they were of the same occupation, tentmakers by trade, he stayed with them and worked. He reasoned in the synagogue every Sabbath and tried to persuade both Jews and Greeks. . . .

After staying for some time, Paul said farewell to the brothers and sisters and sailed away to Syria, accompanied by Priscilla and Aquila. He shaved his head at Cenchreae because of a vow he had taken. When they reached Ephesus he left them there, but he himself entered the synagogue and debated with the Jews. When they asked him to stay for a longer time, he declined, but he said farewell and added, "I'll come back to you again, if God wills." Then he set sail from Ephesus.

On landing at Caesarea, he went up to Jerusalem and greeted the church, then went down to Antioch. After spending some time there, he set out, traveling through one place after another in the region of Galatia and Phrygia, strengthening all the disciples.

Now a Jew named Apollos, a native Alexandrian, an eloquent man who was competent in the use of the Scriptures, arrived in Ephesus. He had been instructed in the way of the Lord; and being fervent in spirit, he was speaking and teaching accurately about Jesus, although he knew only John's baptism. He began to speak boldly in the synagogue. After Priscilla and Aquila heard him, they took him aside and explained the way of God to him more accurately. When he wanted to cross over to Achaia, the brothers and sisters wrote to the disciples to welcome him. After he arrived, he was a great help to those who by grace had believed. For he vigorously refuted the Jews in public, demonstrating through the Scriptures that Jesus is the Messiah.

(ACTS 18:1–4, 18–28)

Priscilla **WAS A GREAT LEADER** in the early church. She and her husband, Aquila, hosted a church in their home in Ephesus. However, she and Aquila did not originally set out to be leaders of a church. Priscilla and Aquila traveled from their home in Italy to Corinth when Jews were forced to leave Rome, only meeting Paul because they held the same occupation as tentmakers. Later, Paul stayed in their home while he was in Corinth.

Working side by side with them, Paul recognized the work ethic of Aquila and Priscilla. Perhaps more importantly, he recognized their gift for hospitality after staying in their home. Therefore, it made sense that when Paul went to Ephesus, Priscilla and Aquila accompanied him and helped him begin a church there.

While Paul continued to travel and spread the gospel, Priscilla and Aquila remained in Ephesus and helped the church grow. During this time Priscilla and her husband heard the teachings of a new preacher named Apollos. Though Apollos knew about Jesus, and taught about Him accurately, he had only been introduced to "John's baptism," which likely means he did not understand the Holy Spirit's role in the gospel message or in the lives of believers—making his message incomplete and incorrect. When they realized this, Priscilla and Aquila had a choice.

They could criticize and mock him publicly, pointing out the ways in which Apollos was wrong. They could ignore him, assuming that someone else's ministry wasn't their business. They could walk away, insecure or resentful that their gifts of hospitality and service paled in comparison to the more showy gifts of preaching and teaching. Or they could treat him as a beloved brother in the faith, pull him aside, and teach him "the way of God more accurately" (Acts 18:26).

As we see in Scripture, Priscilla and Aquila met with Apollos in private and helped him grasp a greater understanding of Jesus and His gospel message. Though she wasn't the renowned orator in the story, Priscilla played a vital role in spreading the Good News and expanding the early church. This small act ended up bearing much fruit, for as Apollos moved on to preach elsewhere, he ended up helping many believers in their faith, and proving in public that Jesus was truly the Messiah.

> PRISCILLA'S SMALL ACT ENDED UP BEARING MUCH FRUIT AND HELPING MANY BELIEVERS IN THE FAITH.

Are you frustrated by the role you've been assigned—in the church, in your workplace, in your family or your community? Do your gifts feel insignificant compared to the flashy gifts of others? Does your work feel repetitive or worthless in the grand scheme of your life or your world? Do you simply assume your role is limited to your job instead of seeing yourself as a representative of the Lord wherever you are? Oh, friend, trust God's plans for you! Just as Paul reminded the church in Corinth, the church is one body made of many parts—and we need every single one of those parts. You are needed.

Indeed, the body is not one part but many. If the foot should say, "Because I'm not a hand, I don't belong to the body," it is not for that reason any less a part of the body. And if the ear should say, "Because I'm not an eye, I don't belong to the body," it is not for that reason any less a part of the body. If the whole body were an eye, where would the hearing be? If the whole body were an ear, where would the sense of smell be? But as it is, God has arranged each one of the parts in the body just as he wanted. (1 Cor. 12:14–18)

Priscilla saw beyond her role as a mere tentmaker and took hold of her ability to help other believers grow in their knowledge of God. You can do this very thing as well. Look for ways God is asking you to invest in the lives of others around you, and help them better know the Lord. You have no idea who you might be affecting, and how many others they may end up influencing with the words you've shared.

Priscilla's actions may seem small, but her faithfulness helped Paul, the greatest missionary of all time, spread the good news. She even influenced and taught leaders of the early church. No matter how small our actions may seem, or how insignificant we assume our "tent-making" role is, we simply cannot imagine all the ways God will use our leadership and faithfulness for His kingdom.

Prayer

God, thank You for the picture You paint for us of the Church as one body. Thank You for the example Priscilla gave us of loving service and trusting the gifts You give us. Thank You for giving us her example in Your Word, so we can learn what leadership looks like. God, I confess that I doubt You sometimes. That sometimes I'm not sure You gave me the right gifts or opened the right doors in my path. Help me trust You, Lord. Help me believe that You have placed me exactly where You need me, and show me how I can best serve You and serve Your people. Help me remember that no action done for You is worthless, that no service given in Your name will be forgotten. Help me, like Priscilla, teach the full gospel to those who come across my path. Thank You for using me to do Your good work, God. Amen.

Lydia

From Troas we put out to sea and sailed straight for Samothrace, the next day to Neapolis, and from there to Philippi, a Roman colony and a leading city of the district of Macedonia. We stayed in that city for several days. On the Sabbath day we went outside the city gate by the river, where we expected to find a place of prayer. We sat down and spoke to the women gathered there. A God-fearing woman named Lydia, a dealer in purple cloth from the city of Thyatira, was listening. The Lord opened her heart to respond to what Paul was saying. After she and her household were baptized, she urged us, "If you consider me a believer in the Lord, come and stay at my house." And she persuaded us. . . .

About midnight Paul and Silas were praying and singing hymns to God, and the prisoners were listening to them. Suddenly there was such a violent earthquake that the foundations of the jail were shaken, and immediately all the doors were opened, and everyone's chains came loose. When the jailer woke up and saw the doors of the prison standing open, he drew his sword and was going to kill himself, since he thought the prisoners had escaped.

But Paul called out in a loud voice, "Don't harm yourself, because we're all here!"

The jailer called for lights, rushed in, and fell down trembling before Paul and Silas. He escorted them out and said, "Sirs, what must I do to be saved?"

They said, "Believe in the Lord Jesus, and you will be saved—you and your household." And they spoke the word of the Lord to him along with everyone in his house. He took them the same hour of the night and washed their wounds. Right away he and all his family were baptized. He brought them into his house, set a meal before them, and rejoiced because he had come to believe in God with his entire household.

When daylight came, the chief magistrates sent the police to say, "Release those men."

The jailer reported these words to Paul: "The magistrates have sent orders for you to be released. So come out now and go in peace."

But Paul said to them, "They beat us in public without a trial, although we are Roman citizens, and threw us in jail. And now are they going to send us away secretly? Certainly not! On the contrary, let them come themselves and escort us out."

The police reported these words to the magistrates. They were afraid when they heard that Paul and Silas were Roman citizens. So they came to appease them, and escorting them from prison, they urged them to leave town. After leaving the jail, they came to Lydia's house, where they saw and encouraged the brothers and sisters, and departed.

(ACTS 16:11–15, 25–40)

Lydia's NAME MAY NOT APPEAR on every single page in the book of Acts, but her actions are monumental in the early church's growth. She was a businesswoman, a "dealer in purple cloth." Since purple dye was expensive, only the wealthy could afford to own purple cloth. She likely had a thriving business and knew many powerful people in the city of Thyatira. Though her influence as a woman was likely limited by cultural norms, Lydia had connections, and her actions affected a lot of people.

Lydia feared the God of Israel, but her belief was not yet complete. When she heard Paul share the Good News about God's Son and His work on the cross, the Lord opened her heart to respond. She believed in Jesus Christ and then led her entire household to believe and be baptized. She was so excited about her new faith that she invited Paul to stay at her home after that, which became the base of operations for the church in Philippi. Her hospitality made a statement that she was not only for Paul, but that she also supported his gospel message and the church he was starting in the area.

We don't know much about Lydia's life before her encounter with Paul, apart from the fact that she sold purple cloth. What's interesting about that encounter, though, is that Lydia wasn't in a temple or a classroom when she heard about Jesus. She was in the middle of her work day. Though most of her day was spent selling purple fabric at the city gate, she likely took a break to sit down near the river where people regularly gathered to pray to the God of Israel, and in this particular gathering, Paul was a guest speaker. In other words, Lydia was simply taking a work break when she learned the Good News, and God providentially lined up her work schedule with a certain apostle's visit to town to bear the news of the gospel. This teaches us that God can meet us anywhere as long as we are open to hearing from Him!

> ## LYDIA'S HOSPITALITY ALLOWED MANY TO COME TO KNOW THE LORD.

Once again, the small actions of a faithful woman provided a home for Paul during his travels, a comfort that allowed him to teach and preach at no cost to those listening. Lydia's hospitality, as well as her leadership and influence in the community, allowed many to come to know the Lord, and her hospitality to Paul was a great example of servanthood. Eventually, she didn't just host Paul; her home became the regular gathering place for all the new believers that came from his ministry!

Have you embraced the full, true gospel? Have you believed in Jesus and asked His forgiveness for your sins? How has that affected your family or your community? How has it affected your work? God can and will meet you inside a church—and outside it, too. He can speak to you at home or at work, and He can use you in those places as well. May we never stop looking for opportunities to hear from God and serve Him, no matter where we find ourselves on the Lord's Day or on any other day of the week. Just as Lydia offered her home, may we offer whatever we have for the Lord's work and church, so that many more may come to know Him.

Prayer

Dear God, is it true? Will You speak to me in this place? Can You use me even here? I'm no expert or scholar; I'm just me. Can You really reach more people because of something I can do? Show me, God! Show me how to help bring the Good News to the people in my life. Show me how I can make a difference in my world. As Lydia offered her home, show me the things in my life You want to use for Your work and Your church. As Lydia used her community influence, show me how to use the spheres of influence I have as well to see Your kingdom advance. Show me how to follow You and serve You. Open my ears and eyes and heart to everything You would have for me, Lord. I am Yours. I love You. Amen.

Lois & Eunice

Paul went on to Derbe and Lystra, where there was a disciple named Timothy, the son of a believing Jewish woman, but his father was a Greek.

(ACTS 16:1)

Timothy WAS PAUL'S PROTÉGÉ, PARTNER in ministry, and friend. He was also the son of a Jewish mother and a Gentile father. Such family dynamics were likely unusual at the time, and it is interesting that Timothy grew up to follow in his mother's faith footsteps. While we cannot know for sure what went on in Timothy's family, we can draw some conclusions from the words of Paul in his letters to Timothy.

Paul, an apostle of Christ Jesus by God's will, for the sake of the promise of life in Christ Jesus:

To Timothy, my dearly loved son. Grace, mercy, and peace from God the Father and Christ Jesus our Lord.

I thank God, whom I serve with a clear conscience as my ancestors did, when I constantly remember you in my prayers night and day. Remembering your tears, I long to see you so that I may be filled with joy. I recall your sincere faith that first lived in your grandmother Lois and in your mother Eunice and now, I am convinced, is in you also. Therefore, I remind you to rekindle the gift of God that is in you through the laying on of my hands. For God has not given us a spirit of fear, but one of power, love, and sound judgment. (2 Tim. 1:1–7)

When Paul wrote to Timothy, encouraging him in his faith and in his ministry, the first thing he mentioned was Timothy's upbringing. In his efforts to bolster Timothy's resolve to spread the gospel and shepherd the church, Paul appealed to Timothy's family legacy of belief. While Paul seemed to view Timothy as his spiritual son, he also acknowledged the great impact Timothy's mother, Eunice, and grandmother, Lois, had in his life.

As Paul mentions later, Lois and Eunice taught Timothy "the sacred Scriptures" (2 Tim. 3:14–15)—something he needed to lean on while in the trenches of ministry in the early church. When Paul first encountered Timothy, he recognized quickly how solid his faith was and how deep his spiritual knowledge ran. In more than one place in the Bible, Paul notes that this was a direct result of Timothy's mom and grandma teaching him. Clearly, he respected the way Lois and Eunice taught Timothy, both in word and deed.

It's possible that Lois and Eunice were unable to teach Timothy as much or as often as they would have liked, since his father was Greek and, therefore, did not believe as they did. They were likely not the only spiritual influences in Timothy's life, for Greeks had their own forms of religious beliefs. But they stayed true to what they knew and believed, and they lived out their faith in their home and in front of young Timothy. Their example, combined with whatever Scriptures and lessons they were able to impart to their son and grandson, created in Timothy a strong foundation upon which God was able to build a ministry that had incredible, lasting effects.

Lois and Eunice may not have led hundreds of people to the Lord. They may not have died for their faith or shared it in a stadium full of people. All we know for sure is that they taught Timothy, their grandson and son, to know and fear the Lord. They were known for their sincere faith, which affected Timothy at a young age, and in turn, influenced the spread of the gospel throughout the first century.

Timothy traveled with Paul throughout the Roman world, sharing the gospel of Jesus Christ. The daily faithfulness of Lois and Eunice to teach Timothy the Scriptures and model genuine faith in front of him influenced many more people than Timothy. Lois and Eunice embraced their spiritual commitment to their son and grandson, and their daily leadership and example allowed many to come to faith in Christ as Timothy walked out the faith they had passed down to him.

> LOIS AND EUNICE EMBRACED THEIR SPIRITUAL COMMITMENT TO THEIR FAMILY, WHICH ALLOWED MANY TO COME TO FAITH.

If you're disappointed with the small influence you have, remember Lois and Eunice. If you're frustrated by competing influences that seem to drown out the message God has given you to share, remember Lois and Eunice. If you wonder how you could possibly be making a difference by leading faithfully in your home, in your small community, in the confines of the place God has led you, remember Lois and Eunice!

When you trust God with His plan for your life, following and serving Him no matter how unexpected or unusual an assignment He gives you, He will use you. Small acts of faith matter in big ways. We never know what God can or will do with our obedience; we just know He requires it. And when we give it, when we follow Him, when we lead others to His truth, we are joining the ranks of women of sincere faith, women quietly doing kingdom work, women like Lois and Eunice.

Prayer

God, thank You for giving us this glimpse into Timothy's upbringing! It's so encouraging to read about the influence his mom and grandma had, simply by living out their faith at home and teaching him as much as they could about You. What a ripple effect their faithfulness and leadership had! To think that they helped change the entire world by teaching their son and grandson about You—without having any idea the effect his ministry would have. It's so incredible to see the way You work, God. Thank You for showing us behind the scenes of the early church.

And, Lord, please help me remember the story of Lois and Eunice when I feel discouraged in my own life. Help me remember that changing one person's life could actually change the world, that obeying You in small acts of faith can turn into something incredible in Your hands. Please take the small offering I have to give, Lord, and multiply it. Use it to bring many to know Jesus. I pray You work around and through the circumstances that frustrate me, so Your will may be done. Thank You, God. Amen.

Deborah

The Israelites again did what was evil in the sight of the LORD after Ehud had died. So the LORD sold them to King Jabin of Canaan, who reigned in Hazor. The commander of his army was Sisera who lived in Harosheth of the Nations. Then the Israelites cried out to the LORD, because Jabin had nine hundred iron chariots, and he harshly oppressed them twenty years.

Deborah, a prophetess and the wife of Lappidoth, was judging Israel at that time. She would sit under the palm tree of Deborah between Ramah and Bethel in the hill country of Ephraim, and the Israelites went up to her to settle disputes.

She summoned Barak son of Abinoam from Kedesh in Naphtali and said to him, "Hasn't the LORD, the God of Israel, commanded you: 'Go, deploy the troops on Mount Tabor, and take with you ten thousand men from the Naphtalites and Zebulunites? Then I will lure Sisera commander of Jabin's army, his chariots, and his infantry at the Wadi Kishon to fight against you, and I will hand him over to you.'"

Barak said to her, "If you will go with me, I will go. But if you will not go with me, I will not go."

"I will gladly go with you," she said, "but you will receive no honor on the road you are about to take, because the LORD will sell Sisera to a woman." So Deborah got up and went with Barak to Kedesh. Barak summoned Zebulun and Naphtali to Kedesh; ten thousand men followed him, and Deborah also went with him.

Now Heber the Kenite had moved away from the Kenites, the sons of Hobab, Moses's father-in-law, and pitched his tent beside the oak tree of Zaanannim, which was near Kedesh.

It was reported to Sisera that Barak son of Abinoam had gone up Mount Tabor. Sisera summoned all his nine hundred iron chariots and all the troops who were with him from Harosheth of the Nations to the Wadi Kishon. Then Deborah said to Barak, "Go! This is the day the LORD has handed Sisera over to you. Hasn't the LORD gone before you?" So Barak came down from Mount Tabor with ten thousand men following him.

The LORD threw Sisera, all his charioteers, and all his army into a panic before Barak's assault. Sisera left his chariot and fled on foot. Barak pursued the chariots and the army as far as Harosheth of the Nations, and the whole army of Sisera fell by the sword; not a single man was left.

(JUDGES 4:1–16)

The **TIME OF THE JUDGES** was a period of great unrest and turmoil in Israel, when "everyone did whatever seemed right to him" (Judg. 21:25). Deborah is the only female judge in Israel's history. She rose up as the judge of God's people when the Israelites had been sold to King Jabin of Canaan. In her role as judge she settled disputes, but she also served as a prophet, hearing from the Lord and relaying His messages to His people.

Deborah served Israel faithfully as its judge, until finally, the Lord called her to come against the Canaanites. God told Barak to gather troops to defeat Sisera, the commander of Jabin's army—a mission Deborah confirmed when she summoned Barak and said, "Didn't the Lord tell you to do this?"

Hearing his calling corroborated by a prophet and judge surely put Barak's mind at ease, giving him the confidence to gather soldiers to fight the king's army. However, though Deborah didn't exhibit any doubt in God's plan, Barak wasn't sure enough to go without her. His reasoning may have been that if Deborah believed strongly enough in God's plan to go to the front lines (and His protection for those who fought), then he would believe, too.

Showing the same faith and leadership she'd exhibited during her time as a judge, Deborah didn't hesitate when Barak made his ultimatum. She gladly went with him (though she did note that his hesitation would mean he would not receive credit for the victory in the end). Together, Deborah and Barak led the Israelites into battle and ultimately victory over their enemies, bringing peace that lasted for decades (Judg. 5:31b).

Have you been given a message from God? Something you feel compelled to share with someone in particular? Is it something that's hard to say and even harder to hear? Don't be scared! As James tells us, God will always answer when we ask Him for wisdom—and He will show you exactly what to say and when to speak up. However, when you do, be prepared to walk beside your brothers and sisters being called by God. Whether it's something uncomfortable you need to say to another believer, or the message of salvation to a nonbeliever, show your faith in God and the message He's entrusted you with. And show your faithfulness by obeying the same exhortation you've imparted to others.

> **BY FEARLESSLY LEADING, DEBORAH DELIVERED ISRAEL AND HELPED THEM TURN BACK TO THE LORD.**

Deborah's leadership in Israel came at a time when Israel needed it most. After her victory she sings a song to the Lord, saying, "when the leaders lead in Israel, . . . blessed be the LORD" (Judg. 5:2). By fearlessly leading Israel against its enemies, both in word and deed, Deborah delivered Israel and, for a time, helped them turn back to the Lord. May we do the same, serving God's people by sharing His message, and linking arms with others as we obey it.

Prayer

Heavenly Father, thank You for giving me a message to share. Thank You for trusting me to be the one to tell people about You. Thank You for believing in me, for believing that I can be brave enough and bold enough to say the things You've laid on my heart. I trust You and believe in You, too. And I know You will give me the courage I need to follow You this way. God, I ask for that courage and also for wisdom, for timing, for soft hearts prepared to hear Your truth when I share it. Help me be brave, Lord, please. And if You ask me to lead by example, I pray that I won't hesitate. I pray that I'll gladly follow You into the fight, just like Deborah. Give me courage, God. Give me wisdom. Give me everything I need to be Your ambassador here on earth. Thank You, Lord. Amen.

DAY 16

Dorcas

In Joppa there was a disciple named Tabitha (which is translated Dorcas). She was always doing good works and acts of charity. About that time she became sick and died. After washing her, they placed her in a room upstairs. Since Lydda was near Joppa, the disciples heard that Peter was there and sent two men to him who urged him, "Don't delay in coming with us." Peter got up and went with them. When he arrived, they led him to the room upstairs. And all the widows approached him, weeping and showing him the robes and clothes that Dorcas had made while she was with them. Peter sent them all out of the room. He knelt down, prayed, and turning toward the body said, "Tabitha, get up." She opened her eyes, saw Peter, and sat up. He gave her his hand and helped her stand up. He called the saints and widows and presented her alive. This became known throughout Joppa, and many believed in the Lord. Peter stayed for some time in Joppa with Simon, a leather tanner.

(ACTS 9:36–43)

Dorcas HAD A REPUTATION. SHE was known in her community for "doing good works and acts of charity," putting her faith into practice by faithfully serving the Lord and leading in ministry. Though we know that we cannot earn salvation through works, we are also told in the book of James that faith without works is dead, like a dead body without a spirit to animate it. In that case Dorcas—and her faith—was fully alive.

Suddenly, though, she was no longer alive. In the midst of her busy life, overflowing with good deeds, Dorcas became sick and passed away. Her faith had been so vibrant and her influence so deeply felt, however, that her friends could not quite believe that she was gone forever. When they heard Peter, who had already performed miracles in the name of Jesus, was in a town nearby, they asked him to come to Dorcas's home.

Peter left immediately, perhaps due to Dorcas's good and widespread reputation or perhaps because of the urgency of her friends' request for help. When he reached Dorcas's home he was met by widows who had experienced her good works in their own lives. Devastated by the loss of such a kind, generous woman—and, probably, saddened by the realization that she'd no longer be able to help them—these widows made every effort to explain to Peter how incredible Dorcas was, showing him the clothes she'd made for them. They had been recipients of great grace and love.

Clearly Dorcas had not just been a hearer of the word, but also a doer, as evidenced by her charity work and the grieving community she left behind. A follower of Jesus, she was truly a disciple and a leader, and even in her bodily death it was clear the Lord was not finished with her on the earth.

Peter responded to her friends' request, coming to visit her while knowing she had died. After hearing from the widows she had sacrificed so much time and energy for, he sent everyone away. Then Peter prayed and commanded Dorcas to get up—and she did! The Lord restored her life, she opened her eyes, and she sat up. A woman who had been known for her works was now known for the miraculous work of God, and many came to believe because of this miracle and her faithfulness.

> DORCAS WAS NOT JUST A HEARER OF THE WORD, BUT A DOER, WHO SHOWS US THAT EVERY TASK ON GOD'S TO-DO LIST IS SIGNIFICANT.

Frequently it may seem like our own good works go unseen and unappreciated. Perhaps you spend your days (and nights) caring for young children or aging parents, performing what you would consider tedious, insignificant duties for people who are unable to express gratitude for your kindness. Or perhaps you consistently find yourself facing opportunities to serve behind the scenes, again—setting up chairs, making phone calls, taking meals, filling coffee cups, washing dishes, folding laundry, filing paperwork, running errands. Don't despair—and don't look at these tasks with disdain. Every part of the body of Christ is necessary, and every task on God's to-do list is significant.

Dorcas could have ignored the need of the widows in her life to serve those with a higher profile. She could have used her sewing skills for profit, or she could have assumed she couldn't possibly make a difference with such a small gift. She could have simply prayed for the widows to find provision; she could have even just tossed a few coins their way and moved on. But Dorcas was a believer. She'd heard about the life of Jesus and wanted to emulate it. She wanted to lay her life down like He did, and offer what she could to help those He came to help. She wanted to put her faith into practice and share the love of God with those around her. So she acknowledged those in need and used the gifts God had given her to help them in a tangible way, serving the Lord faithfully and quietly—but consistently enough that people began to notice and the town simply wasn't the same without her.

If you're always "doing good works," even behind the scenes, it will not go unnoticed forever. Your obedience and faithfulness are helping people find their way back to God right now—and they will tell the story of His goodness in the future. Think of those who would grieve if you were no longer here, helping them and serving God. Think of the testimony your service is to those you help and to those who witness it. Think of the ways that your small acts of laying down your life show off the one huge act of service Jesus performed for all of us on the cross, where He literally laid down His life. Think of how your kind and small moments of service introduce people to a kind and caring God who isn't too big for their little lives or too involved with more important things to consider them significant. Remember that as you care about the small things in someone else's life, you are showing them the God who cares about the small things.

Don't tire of doing good (Gal. 6:9); the Lord sees your labor and will reward your obedience in His timing. And just like Dorcas, you will be known not just for your good deeds but your faithfulness to God and how your life pointed others to Him.

Prayer

Dear God, thank You for giving me the opportunity to serve You by helping others. I know I'm fortunate to have the resources and ability to do specific things—even the small ones—that other people could not do, and I'm grateful You've shown me how to use it all for Your glory. Please sustain me when I grow weary of doing good, Lord, and remind me of how much I love giving back and sharing all You've given me. Please help me live a life overflowing with so much generosity and kindness that anyone who knows me knows You. Use my life and my ministry to show off who You are to those who come in contact with me. Thank You for letting me be part of Your plan to love Your creation, God. I love You. Amen.

WOMEN *of*
FRIENDSHIP

Ruth

During the time of the judges, there was a famine in the land. A man left Bethlehem in Judah with his wife and two sons to stay in the territory of Moab for a while. The man's name was Elimelech, and his wife's name was Naomi. The names of his two sons were Mahlon and Chilion. They were Ephrathites from Bethlehem in Judah. They entered the fields of Moab and settled there. Naomi's husband Elimelech died, and she was left with her two sons. Her sons took Moabite women as their wives: one was named Orpah and the second was named Ruth. After they lived in Moab about ten years, both Mahlon and Chilion also died, and Naomi was left without her two children and without her husband.

She and her daughters-in-law set out to return from the territory of Moab, because she had heard in Moab that the Lord had paid attention to his people's need by providing them food. She left the place where she had been living, accompanied by her two daughters-in-law, and traveled along the road leading back to the land of Judah.

Naomi said to them, "Each of you go back to your mother's home. May the Lord show kindness to you as you have shown to the dead and to me. May the Lord *grant each of you rest in the house of a new husband." She kissed them, and they wept loudly.*

They said to her, "We insist on returning with you to your people."

But Naomi replied, "Return home, my daughters. Why do you want to go with me? Am I able to have any more sons who could become your husbands? Return home, my daughters. Go on, for I am too old to have another husband. Even if I thought there was still hope for me to have a husband tonight and to bear sons, would you be willing to wait for them to grow up? Would you restrain yourselves from remarrying? No, my daughters, my life is much too bitter for you to share, because the Lord's hand has turned against me." Again they wept loudly, and Orpah kissed her mother-in-law, but Ruth clung to her. Naomi said, "Look, your sister-in-law has gone back to her people and to her gods. Follow your sister-in-law."

But Ruth replied:

Don't plead with me to abandon you
or to return and not follow you.
For wherever you go, I will go,
and wherever you live, I will live;
your people will be my people,
and your God will be my God.

Where you die, I will die,
and there I will be buried.
May the LORD punish me
and do so severely,
if anything but death separates you and me.

When Naomi saw that Ruth was determined to go with her, she stopped talking to
her.

The two of them traveled until they came to Bethlehem. When they entered
Bethlehem, the whole town was excited about their arrival and the local women
exclaimed, "Can this be Naomi?"

"Don't call me Naomi. Call me Mara," she answered, "for the Almighty has made
me very bitter. I went away full, but the LORD has brought me back empty. Why do
you call me Naomi, since the LORD has opposed me, and the Almighty has afflicted
me?"

So Naomi came back from the territory of Moab with her daughter-in-law Ruth
the Moabitess. They arrived in Bethlehem at the beginning of the barley harvest.

(RUTH 1)

She **STAYED. RUTH COULD HAVE** left Naomi, her widowed mother-in-law, to fend for herself as she traveled back to her native land. Ruth was a widow herself, and could have gone back to her own people to make a new way in the world, but she stayed. Her commitment to Naomi was so strong that even today, many people quote her words to communicate their own forms of affection, camaraderie, and commitment to those they love.

Not only did Ruth initially commit to stay with her mother-in-law, but after Naomi had lost all hope and was convinced that God had turned His back on her, Ruth stayed faithful to the commitment she made. She stayed by Naomi's side and provided for them when Naomi could not. She took care of Naomi and encouraged her. Ruth followed through with her commitment in the moments that mattered most.

Naomi didn't make it easy. Though desperately grieving the loss of her sons, husbands, and the land that had been home for years, Naomi wanted what was best for her daughters-in-law. She pleaded with Orpah and Ruth to go back to their homelands. They would be more likely to find husbands there than in Bethlehem, and if one thing was clear to Naomi, it was the importance of finding provision. She felt responsible for these women, even if they were only daughters by marriage, and she wanted to take care of them. But she knew that, as a widow, her options for provision were few. So she urged them to go home, to do what made sense, to leave her alone, to find the provision she could not give them somewhere else.

Orpah was saddened, but practical; she reluctantly left Naomi to return home. She knew this move, as sad as it was, was her best shot at finding a husband, which was the way to make it in her world at the time. Ruth, however, wasn't having it. Despite what common sense told her and despite what Naomi insisted, Ruth wasn't going anywhere. As a matter of fact, it seems that Naomi's arguments for her daughters-in-law leaving her just made Ruth more determined. She listened to Naomi's case; she understood the risk and the implications of her choice. But how could she desert this woman she loved, this woman in pain, this woman who was trying so valiantly to care for her?

Naomi's advice proved how much she cared for Ruth. She was willing to face the world empty and alone so her daughters-in-law might have a chance at a full future. Ruth saw the lengths Naomi was willing to go to ensure her safety, and she went further. Instead of Naomi being the one to sacrifice her future, Ruth decided to do this instead. Ruth embodies the type of friend we all want, and more than that, the friend we do have in Christ. He is the one who has stuck with us, to ensure we will have a future and a family. He is the one who will never leave us or forsake us, and who promises to give us a place to belong. Like Ruth, He does not abandon us in the hard moments. He stays and He comforts and He reminds us that we have hope even in the darkest of situations.

> LIKE RUTH, GOD DOES NOT ABANDON US IN THE HARD MOMENTS.

Do you have a friend like Ruth? Has anyone stuck by your side, despite trials and tests? Is there someone in your life that has stood beside you, though time or circumstances or misunderstandings would have sent other friends packing? If you do, praise God! What an enormous blessing to have someone like Ruth who will love you and encourage you and protect you and care for you through the seasons!

But perhaps you haven't experienced friendship like Ruth offered Naomi. Perhaps your friends returned home, in a manner of speaking, when life got hard or when friendship became inconvenient. Oh, friend, that is so hard! And when that's your friendship story, forgiveness can be slow to find, healing even slower. But don't give up. Look to Jesus, your true friend who loves and shows up at all times. Ask Him to first, show Himself as the friend you've been longing for, and second, send you a Ruth friend. Even better? Ask Him to help you be a Ruth friend to a Naomi in your life.

What incredible love these two women shared! What respect they had for the other, even though we see them argue and disregard the other's opinion about their next steps. Ruth was a faithful daughter-in-law, and even more so, a faithful friend. When Naomi was at her lowest point in life, Ruth stayed by her side, just as One who would stay by our side and give us a family in the Lord. God used Ruth's friendship to slowly soften Naomi's heart, and He ultimately blessed Ruth with a son and Naomi with a grandson—a lineage that would eventually lead to the Messiah, the ultimate friend of sinners. May we be the same kind of fiercely loyal friend that Ruth was to Naomi and that Christ is to us, and may God bless our friendships richly, even in hard seasons.

Prayer

Dear Lord, thank You for being my friend. I know that no matter how many times I'm disappointed or deceived or hurt by people, You will never abandon me. You will never lie to me, and You will always want the best for me. Thank You for being fiercely loyal to me the way Ruth was to Naomi. And, God, I pray that You would help me be that same kind of friend. Show me who is hurting, who needs someone to walk with her right now—and show me how to help her! Give me the endurance and the compassion, the love and the courage to take the risk of being a Ruth-friend to someone near me. I love You, Jesus. You are my best friend, and I'm so grateful for You. Teach me to befriend others in their dark seasons, the way You have befriended me, even when others would walk away. Amen.

Elizabeth

In those days Mary set out and hurried to a town in the hill country of Judah where she entered Zechariah's house and greeted Elizabeth. When Elizabeth heard Mary's greeting, the baby leaped inside her, and Elizabeth was filled with the Holy Spirit. Then she exclaimed with a loud cry: "Blessed are you among women, and your child will be blessed! How could this happen to me, that the mother of my Lord should come to me? For you see, when the sound of your greeting reached my ears, the baby leaped for joy inside me. Blessed is she who has believed that the Lord would fulfill what he has spoken to her!"

(LUKE 1:39–45)

Elizabeth WAS NOT SUPPOSED TO have a child. She was well past childbearing years, but the Lord blessed her with a son. It was surprising, yet cause for much rejoicing. Her cousin, Mary, was also not supposed to have a child, but for very different reasons. Mary was too young, and was not married. Being single and bearing a child in her day would have brought on rumors, side glances, and religious judgment and exclusion. Nevertheless, the Lord also blessed her with a son.

As we see in Scripture, Mary quickly understood how blessed she was and praised God for His gift. Both her and Elizabeth's pregnancies were unexpected, but both were divinely inspired; despite the differences in their circumstances, the incredible similarities bonded these cousins. Nothing like a shared experience deepens and strengthens a friendship.

Elizabeth's pregnancy was a surprise; after so many years of infertility, she had long accepted her place in society as a childless woman who, despite her husband's position as priest, was judged less than by her community. The sole purpose of a woman in those times was to have and raise children, to keep the family lineage going for the sake of both security and status. And now, finally, she would receive this honor! Elizabeth's pleasure and relief to be with child surely outweighed the inconvenience (and, likely rumor mill) of her husband's sudden inability to hear or speak. Still, for the first several months of her pregnancy, she stayed home and kept to herself (Luke 1:24–25).

Even before Mary saw her cousin, Elizabeth and her unexpected pregnancy were encouraging Mary. Faced with a brilliant (and probably terrifying) angel with an unbelievable (and, again, probably terrifying) message, Mary was unsure. She asked how she could possibly be pregnant, since she had never been intimate with a man. A reasonable question! The angel explained the supernatural miracle to come but also gave Mary a tangible example in her cousin's story that she could hold onto as she processed her news.

The angel replied to [Mary]: "The Holy Spirit will come upon you, and the power of the Most High will overshadow you. Therefore, the holy one to be born will be called the Son of God. And consider your relative Elizabeth— even she has conceived a son in her old age, and this is the sixth month for her who was called childless. For nothing will be impossible with God."

"I am the Lord's servant," said Mary. "May it be done to me according to your word." Then the angel left her. (Luke 1:35–38)

When her cousin Mary arrived, pregnant herself, Elizabeth rejoiced again. Here was someone who would understand the miracle she was living, someone she could wonder and worship with, someone who would get it. Mary, of course, was facing a different sort of miracle; not all impossible pregnancies are the same. She was young and unmarried, but engaged to a tradesman. Elizabeth, older and wiser, took in her cousin and all her anxieties—and loved her well.

Elizabeth's family, that of a priest, had more luxuries than Mary's might have had. While pampering a weary body is a short-term solution to bigger concerns, both Elizabeth's older body and Mary's young one likely benefited from some comfort during the usual aches and pains that come with carrying a child. With her physical needs cared for, Mary could relax and rest in the care of her cousin, opening her heart to the celebration she knew her baby and her Lord deserved.

Elizabeth became the emotional, spiritual, and physical support that Mary needed in an uncertain time. Elizabeth welcomed Mary into her home and shared her experience with Mary. Elizabeth encouraged Mary and reminded her of the great privilege she had been given. Elizabeth knew the child Mary held in her womb was her Messiah, and celebrated this fact with exuberance. Elizabeth blessed Mary through her belief and encouraged Mary to hold on to her own. Elizabeth's friendship was an incredible gift to a young, uncertain, pregnant girl.

(**BE THE ELIZABETH TO SOMEONE ELSE'S MARY.**)

Many have said that some of the most powerful words are "me, too." When facing a difficult situation, especially one that feels unusual or isolating, learning that someone else has faced something similar provides enormous relief. Seeing that someone else has experienced the same thing—and survived (or even thrived)—can be the difference between putting your head down to endure a certain situation, or walking through it with your head held high. Hearing someone confirm that what you are undergoing is real and hard and understandable can be the biggest gift you receive. Locking arms with another who has already faced what you are facing might make you stronger than you were even before the current situation began. As C. S. Lewis famously said, true friendship arises when two people look at one another and say "What! You too? I thought I was the only one."[1]

Are you going through something difficult right now? Have you just finished going through something hard, really hard? Is it possible that you could offer the same sort of encouragement Elizabeth offered Mary by sharing your experience, by telling someone in the same boat, "me, too"? When life hits us hardest, it's easy to be tempted to keep our heads down, to do our best to simply plod forward and survive. But what if we looked up? What if we looked around, found someone else whose shoulders are bearing the same sort of burden? What if we met her eyes and said, "I get it"? What if we took turns lifting one another's spirits and pointing each other back to the truth? What if we could be the Elizabeth to someone else's Mary?

Prayer

Dear Lord, I cannot imagine having an angel appear to me and announcing that I've conceived the Son of God Himself. Honestly, right now, all I can imagine is this situation I'm in, this thing I'm dealing with today. It's all I can think about, and I'm drowning—in fear, in stress, in loneliness. I feel so alone, God; I definitely can't imagine anyone else knows how I feel. Nobody else knows what this is like . . . do they? Do You know? Is there someone out there who would understand? Lord, if You gave Mary and Elizabeth each other, I know You can give me someone, too. Please show me who I can lean on and let lean on me; please show me who will understand what I'm going through. Thank You, God. Thank You for listening and understanding and for sending me a friend. Please help me be a good friend, too. Show me someone in my life who may need encouragement, who may be undergoing something I've already been through. Send me an Elizabeth, yes. And also make me an Elizabeth to someone else. Amen.

---

1. C. S. Lewis, *The Four Loves* (New York: Harcourt, Brace, 1960), 65.

Mary Magdalene

On the first day of the week Mary Magdalene came to the tomb early, while it was still dark. She saw that the stone had been removed from the tomb. So she went running to Simon Peter and to the other disciple, the one Jesus loved, and said to them, "They've taken the Lord out of the tomb, and we don't know where they've put him!"

At that, Peter and the other disciple went out, heading for the tomb. The two were running together, but the other disciple outran Peter and got to the tomb first. Stooping down, he saw the linen cloths lying there, but he did not go in. Then, following him, Simon Peter also came. He entered the tomb and saw the linen cloths lying there. The wrapping that had been on his head was not lying with the linen cloths but was folded up in a separate place by itself. The other disciple, who had reached the tomb first, then also went in, saw, and believed. For they did not yet understand the Scripture that he must rise from the dead. Then the disciples returned to the place where they were staying.

But Mary stood outside the tomb, crying. As she was crying, she stooped to look into the tomb. She saw two angels in white sitting where Jesus's body had been lying, one at the head and the other at the feet. They said to her, "Woman, why are you crying?"

"Because they've taken away my Lord," she told them, "and I don't know where they've put him."

Having said this, she turned around and saw Jesus standing there, but she did not know it was Jesus. "Woman," Jesus said to her, "why are you crying? Who is it that you're seeking?"

Supposing he was the gardener, she replied, "Sir, if you've carried him away, tell me where you've put him, and I will take him away."

Jesus said to her, "Mary."

Turning around, she said to him in Aramaic, "Rabboni!"—which means "Teacher."

"Don't cling to me," Jesus told her, "since I have not yet ascended to the Father. But go to my brothers and tell them that I am ascending to my Father and your Father, to my God and your God."

Mary Magdalene went and announced to the disciples, "I have seen the Lord!" And she told them what he had said to her.

(JOHN 20:1–18)

Mary MAGDALENE BEHELD THE GREATEST news in all history, but she didn't realize it because it was so unbelievable. When she visited Jesus' tomb that morning, she expected to anoint His dead body with the spices and perfumes she and the other women had prepared. But the stone was rolled away from the entrance of the tomb and His body was gone.

Walking to Jesus' tomb on that Sunday morning, she probably could not have imagined feeling sadder. But when she saw that her Savior's body was not where it was supposed to be, Mary grieved again, and more deeply than ever. Her devastation was so great that when she heard a man inquiring about her tears, she didn't even realize the identity of the one speaking.

Not comforted or calmed by the appearance of two angels in the empty tomb, Mary sobbed at the second loss of her Lord and her friend. When a man asked her why she was crying, she assumed he was the gardener and explained. Literally blinded with grief, she didn't realize the man she spoke to was, indeed, Jesus. That is, until He spoke her name. In that moment, she knew. She knew and she believed, then she celebrated and shared the good news that Jesus had risen.

Have you ever been so consumed with emotion that you missed hearing the voice of God? So upset that even if an angel appeared to you, you wouldn't be able to believe God knew what He was doing? Perhaps you have been filled with such outrage or frustration that you couldn't hear the still, small whisper of God's Spirit offering you peace. Or maybe you have been so overwhelmed with anxiety and fear that you cannot process the grace and hope before your eyes.

We are all susceptible to such human responses, the ones that fill our senses and cause us to stumble and lash out instead of being still and knowing our Lord's voice. Thankfully, God knows this and is patient, waiting while we work through our emotions, saying our name again until we recognize His voice.

> **LIKE MARY, MAY WE SHOUT IT OUT: I HAVE SEEN THE LORD!**

If you're in the midst of a meltdown right now and you can't get a handle on what's true and what's not, breathe in and listen. Look up. Do you see Him? Do you see Him reaching for you, with love in His eyes, ready to comfort and guide you? To assure you that He is bigger than any struggle or loss you face, that He is stronger than any cross or tomb or any other foe? He's there. You just have to look up. And when you do—when you see Him and understand what He's been trying to tell you all along—what will you do with that knowledge?

May we all be like Mary Magdalene, friend to Jesus and witness to His resurrection. May we praise Him and celebrate His miracles—and then shout it out: I have seen the Lord! When Mary Magdalene realized Jesus was standing before her, she left the garden to tell the rest of His disciples what she had seen. Jesus was risen, and she couldn't wait to tell her friends. May we also share the greatest news in history with all who will listen, telling them all the ways He is meeting us in our chaos, drawing near in our woes, and working in our lives.

Prayer

Jesus! You're here! Oh, You're here and I'm so glad. Lord, I was afraid You were gone, that I wouldn't see or hear from You again. I've been so sad, so angry, so confused. The world has felt so dark, and I didn't know what to do. I reached out to You even though I wasn't sure it would matter, because it's all I know to do. And now, here You are, with me like You promised. Thank You! Thank You, God, for fulfilling Your every promise, for never leaving us, for answering my cries. I want to tell everyone about this, Lord. Give me the courage to speak boldly, please. Give me the words to say and show me the ones to say them to. Help me share the ways You have showed up for me, saying my name and drawing near in my darkest moments. And help me share the greatest news of all— the fact that You are real and risen. Thank You, Lord. I love You! Amen.

Queen of Sheba

The queen of Sheba heard about Solomon's fame connected with the name of the
Lord and came to test him with riddles. She came to Jerusalem with a very large
entourage, with camels bearing spices, gold in great abundance, and precious
stones. She came to Solomon and spoke to him about everything that was on
her mind. So Solomon answered all her questions; nothing was too difficult for
the king to explain to her. When the queen of Sheba observed all of Solomon's
wisdom, the palace he had built, the food at his table, his servants' residence, his
attendants' service and their attire, his cupbearers, and the burnt offerings he
offered at the Lord's temple, it took her breath away.

She said to the king, "The report I heard in my own country about your words and
about your wisdom is true. But I didn't believe the reports until I came and saw
with my own eyes. Indeed, I was not even told half. Your wisdom and prosperity
far exceed the report I heard. How happy are your men. How happy are these
servants of yours, who always stand in your presence hearing your wisdom.
Blessed be the Lord your God! He delighted in you and put you on the throne of
Israel, because of the Lord's eternal love for Israel. He has made you king to carry
out justice and righteousness."

Then she gave the king four and a half tons of gold, a great quantity of spices, and
precious stones. Never again did such a quantity of spices arrive as those the
queen of Sheba gave to King Solomon.

In addition, Hiram's fleet that carried gold from Ophir brought from Ophir a
large quantity of almug wood and precious stones. The king made the almug wood
into steps for the Lord's temple and the king's palace and into lyres and harps for
the singers. Never before did such almug wood arrive, and the like has not been
seen again.

King Solomon gave the queen of Sheba her every desire—whatever she asked—
besides what he had given her out of his royal bounty. Then she, along with her
servants, returned to her own country.

(1 KINGS 10:1–13)

The QUEEN OF SHEBA BECAME an incredible blessing to Israel's king, though she was initially suspicious of Solomon's wealth and wisdom. After hearing rumors about him, she traveled to Jerusalem in order to find out if the reports about Solomon were true. As queen it must have been quite an undertaking to travel this great distance simply to satisfy her curiosity. But rather than depending on gossip or reputation, the Queen of Sheba chose to see for herself whether the tales told about King Solomon were more than legend.

When she arrived, the queen was welcomed and allowed access to the king and his court. Completely astonished and overwhelmed by Solomon's wisdom, the queen blessed him with many things, including gold, spices, and precious stones. With these gifts, she showed that she did not take Solomon's time or knowledge lightly. In her time and culture, presenting these gifts of gratitude were the way to reveal that she respected him as a fellow leader and friend, and she appreciated what he so freely gave her.

However, though her gifts were costly and impressive, her greatest gift to Solomon was the encouragement she shared. Some people shower words on others frivolously, oftentimes flattering with empty declarations and compliments; but not the Queen of Sheba. Like a good friend does, she reminded Solomon what was true: that his men and servants were happy and blessed by his wisdom and that God had specifically appointed him to be king over Israel, blessing him with incredible wisdom. She reminded him that it was because of God's great love for Israel that He placed Solomon on the throne.

> LIKE A GOOD FRIEND DOES, THE QUEEN REMINDED SOLOMON WHAT WAS TRUE.

Do you have any friends who need encouragement, who need to be reminded of what's true? Have you heard rumors about her success or her stress? Have you wondered what the real story is? Who in your life could you show appreciation for with the gift of presence, of time, of kind words? The Queen of Sheba didn't put off the opportunity to foster a friendship with King Solomon. She didn't rely on the observation of others—or the promise to get together soon. She also didn't show up, empty-handed and demanding, making a visit all about her needs.

What face comes to mind when we talk about people who may need a kind word? What hurdles could you jump to make time to visit and encourage her?

What began as a monarch's effort to discover the truth behind the legend of another leader resulted in a rich, rewarding friendship. The Queen of Sheba was a wonderful friend to Solomon because she reminded him of what was true. Through her words she reminded him that God had placed him on the throne for a purpose—his place in the world was ordained and important. His wisdom was a great gift from God and this encouragement was a great gift from a friend.

May we be the same kind of friends, setting aside our doubt and cynicism to observe the reality of one another's goodness. May we remember how precious God finds every one of His children and how He has plenty of blessing to go around. May we respect each other's time and life stage, giving and receiving lovely gifts that illustrate our appreciation for one another. May we remain open-minded and soft-hearted as we enter into conversation and even debate, honestly encouraging one another and pointing one another back to God. May we be each other's Queen of Sheba—reminding each other what is true, and helping each other see that our place in this world is ordained and important, just as Solomon's was.

Prayer

Dear God, thank You for my friends—and the work You're doing in their lives. And forgive me for any jealousy or resentment I've felt toward them. Forgive me for assuming they're doing just fine on their own, for believing every rumor I hear or conclusion I draw based what their life seems like from the outside looking in. Lord, I'd love to sit down with a friend, to ask her how she's doing, how she's really doing. Please give me that opportunity. Please open my eyes to see—and seize—every chance to look my friends in the eye, listen to them share about their lives, and notice every single way You are blessing them and working through them. Then give me the courage to say something! Give me the courage to speak up and tell my friend how amazing it is to see how You've blessed her. Help me be the kind of open, giving, encouraging friend the Queen of Sheba was to King Solomon—the kind that shares what's true and reminds others of their place in this world. And thank You for being the best Friend of all. I love You, Lord. Amen.

Naaman's Servant

Naaman, commander of the army for the king of Aram, was a man important to his master and highly regarded because through him, the LORD had given victory to Aram. The man was a valiant warrior, but he had a skin disease.

Aram had gone on raids and brought back from the land of Israel a young girl who served Naaman's wife. She said to her mistress, "If only my master were with the prophet who is in Samaria, he would cure him of his skin disease."

So Naaman went and told his master what the girl from the land of Israel had said. Therefore, the king of Aram said, "Go, and I will send a letter with you to the king of Israel."

So he went and took with him 750 pounds of silver, 150 pounds of gold, and ten sets of clothing. He brought the letter to the king of Israel, and it read:

When this letter comes to you, note that I have sent you my servant Naaman for you to cure him of his skin disease.

When the king of Israel read the letter, he tore his clothes and asked, "Am I God, killing and giving life that this man expects me to cure a man of his skin disease? Recognize that he is only picking a fight with me."

When Elisha the man of God heard that the king of Israel had torn his clothes, he sent a message to the king, "Why have you torn your clothes? Have him come to me, and he will know there is a prophet in Israel." So Naaman came with his horses and chariots and stood at the door of Elisha's house.

Then Elisha sent him a messenger, who said, "Go wash seven times in the Jordan and your skin will be restored and you will be clean."

But Naaman got angry and left, saying, "I was telling myself: He will surely come out, stand and call on the name of the LORD his God, and wave his hand over the place and cure the skin disease. Aren't Abana and Pharpar, the rivers of Damascus, better than all the waters of Israel? Couldn't I wash in them and be clean?" So he turned and left in a rage.

But his servants approached and said to him, "My father, if the prophet had told you to do some great thing, would you not have done it? How much more should you do it when he only tells you, 'Wash and be clean'?" So Naaman went down and dipped himself in the Jordan seven times, according to the command of the man of God. Then his skin was restored and became like the skin of a small boy, and he was clean.

Then Naaman and his whole company went back to the man of God, stood before him, and declared, "I know there's no God in the whole world except in Israel. Therefore, please accept a gift from your servant."

(2 KINGS 5:1–15)

She **WAS A YOUNG ISRAELITE** girl, taken from her home in the land God promised to give her forefathers. More than just being taken, she was forced to be a slave to the commander of the army of Aram, a pagan nation and enemy of Israel. She had every right to be angry and resentful—or perhaps the wiser move for her would have been keeping her head down and avoiding any conflict. Instead, when this young girl noticed that her mistress's husband, Naaman, had a skin disease, she spoke up. She extended grace to her master and even friendship, suggesting a way for Naaman to be cured.

The young servant girl told Naaman to visit the man of God in Israel. Though he didn't quite understand her suggestion at first, Naaman eventually sought out Elisha. When he received instructions from Elisha, via his messenger rather than a face-to-face conversation with the prophet, Naaman became angry. A man of his prominence wasn't used to feeling neglected or ignored, and he definitely didn't like being told the cure was in the water of a foreign river. But again, he was counseled by his servants, possibly including the girl who prompted this journey, and he decided to give Elisha's advice a try. After washing himself seven times in the Jordan River, Naaman was indeed healed. He praised Israel's God and confessed that He was not just *a* god, but the *only* God.

> **THOUGH SHE HAD EVERY RIGHT TO BE ANGRY, SHE EXTENDED GRACE.**

Who are you in this story? Are you the servant girl, possessing unique knowledge that could greatly improve the life of someone who has not necessarily been kind to you? Do you know the cure for what plagues him or her? Are you nervous that offering that information could be viewed badly? Or are you reluctant to help someone who has hurt you or who could be considered your enemy?

Or do you relate with Naaman more, feeling ashamed because you've received kindness from someone you have treated poorly? Has someone offered you friendship and grace, even after you were less than kind to her? Has someone you've judged as unimportant recently given you the solution to your problems or guided you in an unexpected, but fruitful direction?

In either case, let us learn from Naaman and the young servant girl. Unlikely friends, for sure, they illustrate the beautiful ways God can change hearts and lives when we are open to His prompting. When we offer one another kindness even when undeserved, when we accept help from someone we've previously ignored or even harmed, God will move. In fact, He has moved already in His Son—the one who helped His enemies, wounded by sin, to be healed through His own death. Like this servant girl, Jesus spent His ministry in enemy territory, being treated like a nobody. Yet, in His work on the cross, He helped His enemies—those who spat on Him and sought to harm Him—so they could know God and be healed.

Because of his young servant's friendship and kindness, Naaman came to revere and honor God. Her simple suggestion changed not only his health, but the course of his life. This unnamed girl who loved her enemy—and acted like the One who would do the same on the cross—is an incredible example of friendship when it is least deserved. No matter the circumstance, she treated others with kindness and respect, speaking up when there was a chance one of her enemies could see the Lord move and, perhaps, believe in Him.

Prayer

Oh Lord, You are so creative in Your mercy and Your plans! Thank You for opening my eyes to friends I never would have chosen for myself, sisters I never would have reached out to on my own. Forgive me for ignoring and hurting and judging others. Forgive me for the times I made assumptions about others and ignored Your command to love them no matter what. Help me love, Lord. Use me to reflect Your light and draw others near to you. Help me be a friend to my enemies the way this unnamed girl was and the way Christ has been to me. Show me when I can do something that would lead them to see You move, that would lead them to declare that You really are the only God. I love You, Lord. Amen.

WOMEN of HOPE

Sarah

God said to Abraham, "As for your wife Sarai, do not call her Sarai, for Sarah will be her name. I will bless her; indeed, I will give you a son by her. I will bless her, and she will produce nations; kings of peoples will come from her."

Abraham fell facedown. Then he laughed and said to himself, "Can a child be born to a hundred-year-old man? Can Sarah, a ninety-year-old woman, give birth?" So Abraham said to God, "If only Ishmael were acceptable to you!"

But God said, "No. Your wife Sarah will bear you a son, and you will name him Isaac. I will confirm my covenant with him as a permanent covenant for his future offspring. As for Ishmael, I have heard you. I will certainly bless him; I will make him fruitful and will multiply him greatly. He will father twelve tribal leaders, and I will make him into a great nation. But I will confirm my covenant with Isaac, whom Sarah will bear to you at this time next year." When he finished talking with him, God withdrew from Abraham.

(GENESIS 17:15–22)

Abraham **AND SARAH BELIEVED IN** God. How could they not, when He spoke directly to Abraham? Perhaps that intimacy of conversation is what emboldened them to speak so freely with and about the Lord, outright questioning His proclamation that they would have a baby. Both times God promised Sarah would have a baby, a son whose descendants would fill the earth, she doubted. She knew her body was "worn out and old," and the thought of it creating and nurturing a baby was simply too much for her to comprehend.

Even with the benefit of Scripture and hindsight that we have today, it is difficult for us to understand why God kept Sarah barren for so long, only to bless her with a baby in her nineties. A pregnancy in the prime of her childbearing years would not have been unusual; no disbelief would have needed to be suspended in that case. It would simply have been life as normal.

But to believe a promise for decades, in the face of devastating infertility? That was not normal. And to have a baby when her hair was gray and her skin was wrinkled, when her body was not equipped to conceive or feed a baby? Definitely unusual! Without the Lord and His mysterious ways, Sarah and Abraham might not have learned the invaluable lessons of trust and hope.

The LORD said, "I will certainly come back to you in about a year's time, and your wife Sarah will have a son!" Now Sarah was listening at the entrance of the tent behind him.

Abraham and Sarah were old and getting on in years. Sarah had passed the age of childbearing. So she laughed to herself: "After I am worn out and my lord is old, will I have delight?"

But the LORD asked Abraham, "Why did Sarah laugh, saying, 'Can I really have a baby when I'm old?' Is anything impossible for the LORD? At the appointed time I will come back to you, and in about a year she will have a son."

Sarah denied it. "I did not laugh," she said, because she was afraid.

But he replied, "No, you did laugh." (Gen. 18:10–15)

When Sarah heard that she was going to have a child, she laughed. She probably didn't mean to; it was likely a reaction to the preposterous thought that after all these years, after everything they'd gone through, after all the disappointment, she would finally have a baby. Hope is a dangerous thing, after all. It makes you vulnerable as you dare to believe the impossible, as you accept that you may see the blessings you've been promised.

Sarah was almost ninety years old, and she had likely let her hope for a child die over and over again throughout her life. But when the Lord came to visit Abraham and told him Sarah would have a child within the year, Sarah had permission to hope again. Her situation was hard. Both she and her husband were old and worn out. Yet, once again, she clung to hope and the promise God had made to Abraham. As dangerous as it was, her hope was worth it. And in the end, God was right. The lineage that came from Abraham and Sarah grew into a small people group that would eventually give way to the Messiah, who would bring in far more people into the family through his work on the cross.

> **SARAH CLUNG TO HOPE AND THE PROMISE OF GOD.**

What are you hoping for today? What is that thing that you're too afraid to even name, that wish or dream or desire you've buried so deep that you scarcely even remember it (at least during the day)? Perhaps it's the thing that keeps you awake at night or sneaks into your dreams. Perhaps it pops up when you hear that song or smell that flower or see that road sign. What hope feels most dangerous to your heart and mind, to your faith in a good God and loving Father?

Dare to hope that God will answer you according to His good purposes. Breathe out nervous laughter if you must, but breathe in certainty that God loves you. Rest in the knowledge that God answers your prayers every time, and that His response to them is always good. Dare to believe that God hears your cries and feels your pain today, just as He heard the cries of a weary world before sending His Son to fulfill every promise. Dare to trust that His plan is the best one, better than you can even imagine. Dare to hope, against all evidence and doubts and what seems to be true. Dare to hope that God is who He says He is, that He'll do what He says He'll do. Dare to hope like Sarah.

Prayer

Dear God, can this be true? Can you possibly do what I've asked so many times? What I've longed for and cried for and finally accepted will simply never happen? Are You really listening to my petitions, or are You kidding me? I know I probably shouldn't ask that, but God, I'm afraid. I'm afraid to believe for one second, to open myself up again, to hope. I'm afraid that Your answer might not be what I'm hoping for. I'm afraid You might say no again; I'm afraid You might say yes. I don't know which is best—if You would finally say yes to this request and move to bless me in such an incredible way, or if what I'm asking for may not be best in the end. The truth is, I don't know. But I know You do. I know You are in control. I know You love me and that Your promises are true. So God, help me. Help me believe and wait, and help me to hope in Your wisdom and discernment in my situation. Help me trust that You know just the right answer to this. Give me the hope and the faith to keep coming to You with this. Thank You, God. I love You. Amen.

Martha

When Jesus arrived, he found that Lazarus had already been in the tomb four days. Bethany was near Jerusalem (less than two miles away). Many of the Jews had come to Martha and Mary to comfort them about their brother.

As soon as Martha heard that Jesus was coming, she went to meet him, but Mary remained seated in the house. Then Martha said to Jesus, "Lord, if you had been here, my brother wouldn't have died. Yet even now I know that whatever you ask from God, God will give you."

"Your brother will rise again," Jesus told her.

Martha said to him, "I know that he will rise again in the resurrection at the last day."

Jesus said to her, "I am the resurrection and the life. The one who believes in me, even if he dies, will live. Everyone who lives and believes in me will never die. Do you believe this?"

"Yes, Lord," she told him, "I believe you are the Messiah, the Son of God, who comes into the world."

Having said this, she went back and called her sister Mary, saying in private, "The Teacher is here and is calling for you."

As soon as Mary heard this, she got up quickly and went to him. Jesus had not yet come into the village but was still in the place where Martha had met him. The Jews who were with her in the house consoling her saw that Mary got up quickly and went out. They followed her, supposing that she was going to the tomb to cry there.

As soon as Mary came to where Jesus was and saw him, she fell at his feet and told him, "Lord, if you had been here, my brother would not have died!"

When Jesus saw her crying, and the Jews who had come with her crying, he was deeply moved in his spirit and troubled. "Where have you put him?" he asked.

"Lord," they told him, "come and see."

Jesus wept.

So the Jews said, "See how he loved him!" But some of them said, "Couldn't he who opened the blind man's eyes also have kept this man from dying?"

Then Jesus, deeply moved again, came to the tomb. It was a cave, and a stone was lying against it. "Remove the stone," Jesus said.

Martha, the dead man's sister, told him, "Lord, there is already a stench because he has been dead four days."

Jesus said to her, "Didn't I tell you that if you believed you would see the glory of God?"

So they removed the stone. Then Jesus raised his eyes and said, "Father, I thank you that you heard me. I know that you always hear me, but because of the crowd standing here I said this, so that they may believe you sent me." After he said this, he shouted with a loud voice, "Lazarus, come out!" The dead man came out bound hand and foot with linen strips and with his face wrapped in a cloth. Jesus said to them, "Unwrap him and let him go."

(JOHN 11:17–44)

Martha WAS BESIDE HERSELF WITH grief, stripped of any propriety or manners. Her beloved brother had died. She had sent word to Jesus, the only one who could save Lazarus, and He had not come in time. So when He finally arrived, Martha ran to meet Him, crying about what she saw as Jesus' missed opportunity to save her brother. She just knew that everything would be different if only Jesus had come sooner.

"If only . . ." is the door to a downward spiral of bitterness and resentment, but Martha stopped short of walking through it. She expressed her deep sadness to Jesus, but then followed it up with her belief in Jesus' power. Leaning into her faith in an all-knowing, all-loving, all-powerful God, she asked Jesus to help her understand her circumstances. She stopped her "if only" from growing into something bigger by reminding herself of a bigger truth: "yet even now." Even in the worst moment imaginable, she knew Jesus could still work. She knew He was God's Son, and that whatever He asked the Father would be granted to Him. In the presence of her friend and her Lord, she remembered that no matter what happened, God is good and loving and powerful, and Jesus has the ability to change things.

> **EVEN IN THE WORST MOMENT IMAGINABLE, MARTHA KNEW JESUS COULD STILL WORK.**

Even in the midst of incredible loss, Martha clung tightly to the hope she had in her Lord. She knew that Jesus could have saved her brother, and she didn't understand why He hadn't. But, she was also sure that Jesus was able to do anything and that He was the Messiah. Martha's hope was not in the result of her situation, but in the One who held her brother's life as well as her own. Her hope was in the person of Christ, the Messiah, despite the horrible situation happening around her. She certainly communicated her desire to see her brother restored, but she was able to accept any result because her hope lay in her Savior, not the outcome.

Jesus ended up raising her brother to life as a picture of His own resurrection to come. Martha got to be a part of this miraculous moment simply because she ran to Jesus in her pain, and she had hope in His plan, whatever it was.

Are you surrounded by a horrible situation right now? Are you facing a dead end, the death of a dream or business or relationship or life? Are you wondering, even if you don't say it out loud, where God was when everything fell apart? Friend, Jesus hears you and feels deeply for you. Though He knew He would raise Lazarus from the dead, the reality of His friends' grief caused Him enough pain that He wept. Does He not care for you that much? Does He not have that much compassion for you? He does. He loves you and does not enjoy watching you experience the effects of sin and suffering in this world. He wants to comfort you and remind you that He is still good. He wants to reassure you that He still loves you, and that He can—and will—do all things for your good and His glory. Regardless of what is causing you pain, you can rest in the knowledge that God loves you and the hope that He will answer your prayers and dry your tears. Don't live in the "if only God cared" frame of mind. Remember the God who brings dead things to life, and invite Him to breathe fresh life into the decaying situation that you are struggling with "yet even now."

Prayer

God, things are bad right now. I am so sad and angry and disappointed and frustrated. And I'm confused, Lord. Why didn't You stop this from happening? How can You possibly turn this into something good? I don't understand. But I know You do. I know all things are possible with You, and I believe that You love me. So even though I don't know what You will do next, I am hopeful that You will do what's best. You are the Christ who brought Lazarus back from the dead—the one who resurrected yourself! I believe You can bring life to any dead thing, including my situation. Thank You, God, for Your comfort in times of grief and Your promises for all time. Thank You for the work You're going to do here. Amen.

DAY 24

Hagar

Abram's wife Sarai had not borne any children for him, but she owned an Egyptian slave named Hagar. Sarai said to Abram, "Since the Lord has prevented me from bearing children, go to my slave; perhaps through her I can build a family." And Abram agreed to what Sarai said. So Abram's wife Sarai took Hagar, her Egyptian slave, and gave her to her husband Abram as a wife for him. This happened after Abram had lived in the land of Canaan ten years.

He slept with Hagar, and she became pregnant. When she saw that she was pregnant, her mistress became contemptible to her. Then Sarai said to Abram, "You are responsible for my suffering! I put my slave in your arms, and when she saw that she was pregnant, I became contemptible to her. May the Lord judge between me and you."

Abram replied to Sarai, "Here, your slave is in your hands; do whatever you want with her." Then Sarai mistreated her so much that she ran away from her.

The angel of the Lord found her by a spring in the wilderness, the spring on the way to Shur. He said, "Hagar, slave of Sarai, where have you come from and where are you going?"

She replied, "I'm running away from my mistress Sarai."

The angel of the Lord said to her, "Go back to your mistress and submit to her authority." The angel of the Lord said to her, "I will greatly multiply your offspring, and they will be too many to count."

The angel of the Lord said to her, "You have conceived and will have a son. You will name him Ishmael, for the Lord has heard your cry of affliction. This man will be like a wild donkey. His hand will be against everyone, and everyone's hand will be against him; he will settle near all his relatives."

So she named the Lord who spoke to her: "You are El-roi," for she said, "In this place, have I actually seen the one who sees me?" That is why the well is called Beer-lahai-roi. It is between Kadesh and Bered.

So Hagar gave birth to Abram's son, and Abram named his son (whom Hagar bore) Ishmael. Abram was eighty-six years old when Hagar bore Ishmael to him.

(GENESIS 16)

Oh, **HAGAR! OUT OF ALL** the heartbreaking stories in the Bible, hers is one of the most wrenching. This woman lived in a foreign land, as a slave. And because her mistress could not get pregnant and would not wait for the Lord's blessing, Hagar was forced to be intimate with her mistress's husband, Abram, until she became pregnant. Then, once she'd been used to bear Abram a son, her relationship with Sarai—unsurprisingly—fell apart.

It's hard to imagine a scenario in which two women, both married to the same man, one unable to get pregnant and one carrying his son, could continue to live together peacefully. It's much too easy to imagine the snide remarks and insults that flew between the two, escalating to the point that Sarai turned to her husband for support.

With Abram's permission to deal with her slave however she saw fit, Sarai then mistreated Hagar so badly that Hagar could not stand it. She did not believe anyone would help her, and she could not find any relief from her situation. Believing her only option was to run, Hagar fled from Abram and Sarai.

The angel of the Lord found her in the desert, on the road to Shur and, likely, on the way to overwhelming fear and bitterness. He promised Hagar that the Lord had heard her misery and that she was to name her child Ishmael. The Lord's promise gave Hagar hope—hope that God had a plan in this mess, hope that life wouldn't be unbearably hard forever, hope that she wasn't alone. She chose to cling to that hope and the provision the Lord would give her, confident that the child she bore was part of His plan. The Lord's promise gave her the hope, confidence, and strength she needed to return to Abram and Sarai and give birth to the child she carried.

> **HAGAR CHOSE TO CLING TO THE PROVISION THE LORD PROMISED HER.**

Perhaps you're facing difficulty that feels unbearable. Perhaps you've been used or abused, left alone and unloved. Maybe you found yourself in a bad situation—and made it worse. Perhaps the promises you were made turned out to be false, or maybe the gifts you were offered were rescinded. Let Hagar's story encourage you! Though she had a child with her mistress's husband, though she provoked her mistress until her abuse was returned, though she ran away from her problems—God didn't turn away from Hagar. Take heart from God's faithfulness to Hagar, and share her hope in Him. God's promises are always true and will always be fulfilled. They will meet you in the hard place—even if you are running away—just as the angel met Hagar with God's promise right in the middle of her wandering. They will always provide real hope despite the circumstance.

Prayer

Oh God, I have messed up. I have committed sins, and I have had sins committed upon me. It's a mess, and I am miserable. The consequences of all this sin are too much to bear, and I don't think I can handle it. How could I? I'm alone, Lord. And I don't see an end to this pain. I just don't think it's ever going to get better. God! It's not fair. What others have done to me is so much worse than anything I ever did. What did I do to deserve this? Where are You? Have You forgotten me? Will You ever help me?

Okay. I remember now. You will never forget me. You always see me. And You will be with me as I face this situation. I know that, Lord, but please help me remember it. It's so hard, but I know that it's true. Thank You for being with me, no matter my sins or my doubts. Help me hope and trust and believe, Lord. Help me love You more, and lead me to the promises in Your Word that will see me through this time. I believe that they will meet me in this hard place just as Your promises met Hagar in her hard place. Amen.

Anna

When the eight days were completed for his circumcision, he was named Jesus—the name given by the angel before he was conceived. And when the days of their purification according to the law of Moses were finished, they brought him up to Jerusalem to present him to the Lord (just as it is written in the law of the Lord, Every firstborn male will be dedicated to the Lord) and to offer a sacrifice (according to what is stated in the law of the Lord, a pair of turtledoves or two young pigeons).

There was a man in Jerusalem whose name was Simeon. This man was righteous and devout, looking forward to Israel's consolation, and the Holy Spirit was on him. It had been revealed to him by the Holy Spirit that he would not see death before he saw the Lord's Messiah. Guided by the Spirit, he entered the temple. When the parents brought in the child Jesus to perform for him what was customary under the law, Simeon took him up in his arms, praised God, and said,

Now, Master,
you can dismiss your servant in peace,
as you promised.
For my eyes have seen your salvation.
You have prepared it
in the presence of all peoples—
a light for revelation to the Gentiles
and glory to your people Israel.

His father and mother were amazed at what was being said about him. Then Simeon blessed them and told his mother Mary: "Indeed, this child is destined to cause the fall and rise of many in Israel and to be a sign that will be opposed—and a sword will pierce your own soul—that the thoughts of many hearts may be revealed."

There was also a prophetess, Anna, a daughter of Phanuel, of the tribe of Asher. She was well along in years, having lived with her husband seven years after her marriage, and was a widow for eighty-four years. She did not leave the temple, serving God night and day with fasting and prayers. At that very moment, she came up and began to thank God and to speak about him to all who were looking forward to the redemption of Jerusalem.

(LUKE 2:21–38)

Anna **HAD LIVED A LONG** life, much of it alone. After being married just seven years her husband died, leaving her a widow. At that difficult point in her life Anna could have given up all hope in God's plans. Or she could have devoted her hope to searching and waiting for a new husband.

Instead, she devoted her life to seeking, serving, and waiting on the Lord. Hope kept her going when she had nothing else. When the Jews were oppressed in their own land, treated as foreigners and second-class citizens, Anna clung to her hope. She believed God would send the deliverer He'd promised and would save His people from their sins. When Anna heard Simeon's testimony about Jesus at the temple, she too began to praise God and tell all who were around about the coming redemption.

Scripture doesn't tell us much about Anna, but she is called a prophetess. Some say that this could mean God used this woman to begin speaking to His people again, after centuries of silence. Others say it could simply mean that she had a strong enough understanding of the Scriptures to teach the younger women, telling them what God has said in generations past. Either way, she was credited with hearing and knowing the Word of God, and sharing it with others.

Anna also spent years at the temple, praying and fasting and serving. What was she waiting for in all those years? The Messiah. The promised Savior. Like Simeon, she believed He would come and it seems she intended to be there when He did. And sure enough, when Mary and Joseph took Jesus to be presented to the Lord and to offer a sacrifice as their tradition required, they took Him to the very temple where Simeon waited and Anna hoped. And when Anna saw this amazing answer to all her years of prayer, she did what she'd always done, sharing the good news with all.

> **WHEN ANNA SAW THIS AMAZING ANSWER TO PRAYER, SHE SHARED THE GOOD NEWS WITH ALL.**

Have you been waiting for an answer to prayer for a long time? Does it feel as if you've been waiting and praying for eighty-four years? Do you wonder if God is even listening? Are you nervous that perhaps you misunderstood God's promises, that maybe your hope is in vain? Be strong, sister! Cling to the hope that we are given in Scripture and lean on the promises God gives us throughout His Word. And while you wait, with hope and expectation, stay faithful. Serve God while you wait on Him to move; tell everyone you can about your hope and why you've placed it in Him. Pray, fast, serve, and hope—and when God shows up just as He promised He would, celebrate and praise Him and tell everyone what He's done!

Anna held tightly to her hope. She believed God when He said He would send a Messiah to deliver Israel, remaining at the temple day and night, praising God, fasting, and offering up prayers. She was there so often that hoping and waiting for the Messiah seemed to be her favorite pastime. Hope showed where her confidence was, which was in the Lord. She believed in what He said and waited expectantly for Him to fulfill His promise in His time. May our hope remain as steady as Anna's when we wait on the Lord. May we look in His Word for the things He has told us, and believe they will happen in His good time.

Prayer

God, I'm here. Even though part of me wants to run away and hide, I'm here and I'm waiting on You. Because I trust You. I trust You and believe Your promises, and I will wait on You. But God, I'm going to need Your help. Please, help me believe; help me trust You. Help me stay hopeful and expectant; protect me from cynicism and bitterness. Give me patience to wait as long as I need to; give me work and purpose serving you while I wait. Like it was for Anna, my hope is in You, Lord, and Your promises. I couldn't go on without it, without You. Thank You for Your promises. Thank You for never forgetting me. Thank You for being my anchor and my hope. Amen.

The Bleeding Woman

Now a woman suffering from bleeding for twelve years had endured much under many doctors. She had spent everything she had and was not helped at all. On the contrary, she became worse. Having heard about Jesus, she came up behind him in the crowd and touched his clothing. For she said, "If I just touch his clothes, I'll be made well." Instantly her flow of blood ceased, and she sensed in her body that she was healed of her affliction.

At once Jesus realized in himself that power had gone out from him. He turned around in the crowd and said, "Who touched my clothes?"

His disciples said to him, "You see the crowd pressing against you, and yet you say, 'Who touched me?'"

But he was looking around to see who had done this. The woman, with fear and trembling, knowing what had happened to her, came and fell down before him, and told him the whole truth. "Daughter," he said to her, "your faith has saved you. Go in peace and be healed from your affliction."

(MARK 5:25–34)

Twelve YEARS. FOR TWELVE YEARS this woman had suffered, bleeding without relief. Because women were considered unclean during their menstrual cycles during ancient times, it's likely she had spent those years not just weak and possibly in pain, but shunned and isolated, with no one willing to touch her or come near. Desperation had sent her to doctor after doctor through the years, but not one had been able to help her. Instead, we're told, her condition had gotten worse.

Though we don't know what treatment this woman had been given in her pursuit of healing, we know that she had "endured much" and was sicker than ever before. The treatment for her affliction may have actually been just as harmful as her illness itself, and yet her desperation pushed her to continue seeking out a remedy. By the time she heard about Jesus she was likely weak, discouraged, and afraid. But this didn't stop her from trying one more time.

Used to being unseen, unwanted, and untouchable, the woman did not approach Jesus. She did not look Him in the eye and ask for help. She did not cry out in her pain, begging for help. A leader and teacher like Him knew full well He could not come near someone unclean, so she probably assumed. Instead of inviting Him near her, she kept to the shadows, walking behind Him and reaching out, merely touching His clothing for help, and probably hoping He would not notice. In that moment she found the strength to hope again, to reach for the help she so dreadfully needed, and to believe that healing might still be possible. That hope led her to the Savior and Healer, the only One who could give her true relief.

Her hope—and maybe her healing—gave the woman courage. When Jesus felt power leave Him, He asked who had touched Him. The woman did not hide or run away, though she may have wanted to out of habit. Instead, she fell on her knees before her Healer and Savior and confessed. She didn't know how He would react or what He would do to her, but she had integrity and respect for the One who had finally cured her disease. What a relief it must have been when Jesus looked at her and simply said, "Daughter, your faith has saved you."

Perhaps you, too, are suffering an affliction that keeps you isolated and seems incurable. Perhaps you have struggled with something for years—physical or emotional or spiritual or relational—seeking help around every corner but finding no relief at all. Maybe you've been fighting a battle for so long that you've traded your determination and desperation for resignation and resentment. Don't give up hope, friend! Don't settle for distance between you and the Lord; don't begin believing that isolation is all there is for you.

The beauty of the bleeding woman's story is that it illustrates how ready Jesus is to heal us. He doesn't require us to make a formal request; He doesn't demand that we make payments or promises. He simply wants us to reach out to Him with hope. If we reach out to Him, like the woman of this story reached for His clothing, He will respond. His reaction to our faith and need is reflexive; our faith in His ability to step in activates a loving response from Him every time. He may not heal us in the timing or in the way that we assume is best, but He will not ignore us. He will not leave us bleeding in the road. He will respond to us with grace and peace and help when we need it most.

> THE BLEEDING WOMAN'S STORY SHOWS US JESUS SIMPLY WANTS US TO REACH OUT TO HIM WITH HOPE.

After years of suffering, after spending everything she had, after being disappointed over and over, this woman still had hope. She still believed that the man she'd heard of, the one teaching and performing miracles, could help her. She still had enough faith to brave a crowd, a reprimand, and another letdown. And this time, it was worth it. Her hope for healing led to her faith in the Healer, and she found freedom from all her afflictions that day. May we be as bold in our belief and as hopeful in our pursuit of help and care from the Lord.

Prayer

Oh God, I need Your help. I am so tired, so worn out, so exhausted from fighting this battle. Please, Lord, give me the power to bear this. Heal me. Help me! I have tried everything I could think of to fix the problem, but it just keeps getting worse. God, I know I should have come to You first. I just thought I could figure it out on my own, but I realize now I was wrong. I'm making a mess of everything, and I've just about lost everything—all because I don't know how to make this stop. Asking for help is so embarrassing, but even humbling myself to do that hasn't made a difference. Nobody can help me; nobody can fix this. But . . . maybe You can? Maybe You will? I reach out to you today, just as the bleeding woman did. Lord, please bring Your help and care and healing to this issue in my life. Please fix what is broken. Give me strength. Help me. Thank You, God. Amen.

WOMEN *of* HOSPITALITY

DAY 27

Mary (Sister of Lazarus)

While they were traveling, he entered a village, and a woman named Martha welcomed him into her home. She had a sister named Mary, who also sat at the Lord's feet and was listening to what he said. But Martha was distracted by her many tasks, and she came up and asked, "Lord, don't you care that my sister has left me to serve alone? So tell her to give me a hand."

The Lord answered her, "Martha, Martha, you are worried and upset about many things, but one thing is necessary. Mary has made the right choice, and it will not be taken away from her."

(LUKE 10:38–42)

The **STORY OF MARY AND** Martha is well known. Jesus counted the two sisters as friends, and He visited their home more than once. On this occasion Martha found herself attending to all the tasks of hosting Jesus and those who traveled with Him alone, because her sister had abandoned her chores to sit at their guest's feet and listen to Him teach. Martha got frustrated and complained to Jesus; He in turn corrected her and said Mary was actually doing the better thing.

When this short story is discussed, attention is more often given to Martha's misplaced priorities than to Mary's choices. While Martha often gets both credit and criticism for preparing the house for guests, we're told Mary understood the true meaning of hospitality. But how can that be? Why was it better to sit and visit with her guests than to cook or clean or otherwise prepare for them? Just as a close look at Jesus' response to Martha reveals a troubled heart, examining Mary's interaction with Jesus can explain much as well.

Martha was busy preparing the house and the meal for their guests, but as she walked back and forth between rooms, she probably still heard some of her guests' conversation. She may have even been anxious to finish her work· so she could hear more, but the reality of her busyness meant that she missed things. She didn't hear all of what Jesus had come to share that day, and she didn't have time to ask questions or clarify anything she didn't immediately understand from His teaching. She might have been interested in what Jesus had to say, but she was busy and she was distracted.

Mary, on the other hand, wasn't willing to take the chance of missing something from the Messiah. Though she could find comfort in her friendship with Jesus, she also knew Him well enough to realize that He was in the midst of an intense ministry season. As a result, she didn't know when she'd see Him next; she didn't know if she would have another chance to soak up His wisdom and teachings. So rather than risk missing out on something important He had to say, she sat right down at His feet and focused on Him—the formal posture of a Rabbi's disciple in that culture. She absorbed as much time as she could with her Lord, a guest in her home. Sitting at Jesus' feet communicated that she wanted to be more than His host, though that was a privilege; she wanted to be His disciple, His follower for life.

While at first glance it seems that Martha is more concerned with being hospitable, Mary had it right. Instead of worrying about the condition of her home, she was concerned with the condition of her guests. She focused on those who had come to visit her, enjoying spending time with them. Mary sat at Jesus' feet soaking up His every word. She didn't want to miss a moment with Him because she was frantically preparing a meal or sweeping the floor. Jesus commended her for her focus and understanding. Mary's example of hospitality displays grace and confidence. She knew that it didn't matter what her house looked like if her heart was not right.

> MARY SAT AT JESUS' FEET SOAKING UP HIS EVERY WORD. SHE DIDN'T WANT TO MISS A MOMENT WITH HIM.

When we imagine the faces of Martha and Mary on this day, it becomes clear why Mary's choice was the better one. Martha's eyes were surely darting all around, looking for tasks to complete or confirming that the work she'd delegated had been completed. As she hustled from one room to another, catching snippets of Jesus' teaching in between chores, her face was probably turned down, focusing on matters at hand (rather than matters of the heart). Mary, on the other hand, knelt to the floor, looking up at Jesus. She couldn't look away, so full was her devotion to Him and her commitment to listening to Him speak.

How do you greet guests in your home? Do you give them a quick hello and rush back to the kitchen, working furiously to make sure everything is just so? Or do you slow down and enter into conversation with them as they enter into your home?

And what about time with Jesus? Is your quiet time a race to the finish, as you check off one more task for the day? Do you ever find yourself so busy serving on a Sunday morning that, later, you can't remember what the sermon was about? Our hearts and our homes are meant to be open, warm, and welcoming—to each other and to our Lord. May we raise our eyes and our hearts to Jesus like Mary, rather than allowing ourselves to become distracted by the things of this world.

Prayer

Thank You, Jesus, for calling me friend and for wanting to spend time with me. I know You care more about my heart than my cooking or decorating. I know You are asking me to slow down, to pay attention, to lean in and look up into Your face. It's hard to remember, though! Oh, forgive me for getting caught up in work, Lord, for becoming busy and distracted when all You're asking for is my heart and my attention. I want to welcome You and to welcome others—into my home but also into my heart, free of the rush and pressure of hosting and, instead, full of the love and warmth of friendship. Lord, You tell us there's a time for everything, and I ask that You show me the time for tasks and the time for people. Help me know when it's time to set things aside and focus on people instead. Help me be the kind of hostess—and more, the disciple—that Mary was when she sat at Your feet. Lead my focus and attention toward You in a world that fights to keep it on other things. Convict me when I'm settling for snippets from You instead of hearing everything You would want to say to me each day. Thank You, God, for being a teacher and friend who wants to come into my life and speak to me. Amen.

The Shunammite Woman

One day Elisha went to Shunem. A prominent woman who lived there persuaded him to eat some food. So whenever he passed by, he stopped there to eat. Then she said to her husband, "I know that the one who often passes by here is a holy man of God, so let's make a small, walled-in upper room and put a bed, a table, a chair, and a lamp there for him. Whenever he comes, he can stay there."

One day he came there and stopped at the upstairs room to lie down. He ordered his attendant Gehazi, "Call this Shunammite woman." So he called her and she stood before him.

Then he said to Gehazi, "Say to her, 'Look, you've gone to all this trouble for us. What can we do for you? Can we speak on your behalf to the king or to the commander of the army?'"

She answered, "I am living among my own people."

So he asked, "Then what should be done for her?"

Gehazi answered, "Well, she has no son, and her husband is old."

"Call her," Elisha said. So Gehazi called her, and she stood in the doorway. Elisha said, "At this time next year you will have a son in your arms."

Then she said, "No, my lord. Man of God, do not lie to your servant."

The woman conceived and gave birth to a son at the same time the following year, as Elisha had promised her.

(2 KINGS 4:8–17)

The UNNAMED WOMAN FROM SHUNEM understood hospitality. She was well off, but gave to others out of her resources. On her own accord she renovated her home to create better accommodations for Elisha, who she knew to be a man of God.

We aren't told her motivations for this generous act. It's possible that she saw his connection to the divine and selfishly assumed that proximity to such a holy man would lead to blessings for her and her household. It's possible that she was genuinely interested in the God of Israel, and wanted the chance to learn from one of his prophets on a regular basis. After all, God only spoke to His people through His prophets at this time in history, and she had no other way of hearing what He might say. It's also possible that she simply saw a man who traveled by her home often, and needed help in his journey. Regardless of why, it's clear that she provided a comfortable place for Elisha to stay, and she is to be commended for recognizing his need and taking action to meet it.

Even more remarkable than the extreme measures she took to convert part of her home into a space for guests is the Shunammite woman's offer for Elisha to stay with her and her husband any time he was in the area. An open-ended offer, with no strings attached, was a gift indeed. Then, when Elisha felt compelled to give her something in return for her kindness, she declined to ask for a specific gift, hinting that she may not have done this gracious deed for selfish reasons after all. It was only thanks to Elisha's attendant that he realized she was on the brink of losing all the provision and care that she currently had in her life, for her husband was going to pass away soon, and she had no son. In their culture at the time, Elisha's attendant knew that without a close male relative, she'd soon be destitute. So he suggested that she might be blessed by a son.

Because of her wonderful hospitality, Elisha wanted to do something for her. He told her she would have a son—and, much to her surprise and delight, she did. A few years later, her son suddenly died, but through Elisha, the Lord brought him back to life (2 Kings 4:14–37). When she went to Elisha for help, she was confident he could do what she asked. However, in her anguish she reminded Elisha that she'd been hesitant about his claim that she'd have a child in the first place. While she did not hesitate to look for ways to serve the holy man, she'd been reluctant to hope for the thing she'd been missing for so long. So when it seemed as if fate had stolen her son, she went straight to the prophet who had promised her otherwise to set the situation straight.

> SHE WAS NOT AFRAID TO EXTEND HOSPITALITY TO THOSE WHO NEEDED IT.

The Shunammite woman may have been afraid to ask for a son, but she was not afraid to extend hospitality to those who needed it. She welcomed Elisha and his servant with open arms and gave them everything they needed while they stayed with her. She displayed a true heart of hospitality—and did it with a boldness that indicates a strong faith and commitment to serving others. Even her initial refusal of a gift from Elisha and her later demand that he bring her son back to life demonstrate her confidence in God's provision.

Like the Shunammite woman paid attention to the man of God "passing by," we must remember that the Lord is still "passing by" our lives, and we must ask ourselves, are we willing to make room for Him? We assume He is going about

His work "out there" in the world, but do we invite Him "in here," offering Him a place in our hearts and home? Do we believe that He has something to teach us, right here and right now, while He goes about His work in the world?

The renovation in the Shunammite woman's home was likely costly. She had to move things around to make room for the man of God. And the ways in which we make room for God in our own lives will be costly, too. Making room for the Lord and for others will require our time, attention, energy, and resources. Inviting God in our everyday lives will interrupt our schedule and our budgets and our expectations. But when we do make room for the Lord and His people, we will be deeply blessed.

Being hospitable to God and His people is not always perfect, but it is always necessary—and all of us are called to it. The people of God must be willing to welcome and help one another, leaning on His provision and guidance. May we always offer a warm and open welcome to the Lord and to one another, using our resources to provide what others need before they even ask for it.

Prayer

Dear Lord, I want to be as generous as the Shunammite woman! I want to make room for You and for others in my life. Even though it's hard to trust You to provide for all of my needs—especially if I offer part of what I have to someone else, I know You will. I remember how You clothe the lilies of the field and feed the birds of the sky, and I know, Lord, that You will take care of my every need and every barrier that has held me back from hospitality until now. Give me the opportunity to serve You by serving Your people. Show me exactly who to invite into my home and my life, starting with You, and give me the courage and the resources to do so. Thank You, Lord. Thank You for letting me play a part in Your plans and for helping me along the way. Amen.

Esther

Some time later, when King Ahasuerus's rage had cooled down, he remembered Vashti, what she had done, and what was decided against her. The king's personal attendants suggested, "Let a search be made for beautiful young virgins for the king. Let the king appoint commissioners in each province of his kingdom, so that they may gather all the beautiful young virgins to the harem at the fortress of Susa. Put them under the supervision of Hegai, the king's eunuch, keeper of the women, and give them the required beauty treatments. Then the young woman who pleases the king will become queen instead of Vashti." This suggestion pleased the king, and he did accordingly.

In the fortress of Susa, there was a Jewish man named Mordecai son of Jair, son of Shimei, son of Kish, a Benjaminite. He had been taken into exile from Jerusalem with the other captives when King Nebuchadnezzar of Babylon took King Jeconiah of Judah into exile. Mordecai was the legal guardian of his cousin Hadassah (that is, Esther), because she had no father or mother. The young woman had a beautiful figure and was extremely good-looking. When her father and mother died, Mordecai had adopted her as his own daughter.

When the king's command and edict became public knowledge and when many young women were gathered at the fortress of Susa under Hegai's supervision, Esther was taken to the palace, into the supervision of Hegai, keeper of the women. The young woman pleased him and gained his favor so that he accelerated the process of the beauty treatments and the special diet that she received. He assigned seven hand-picked female servants to her from the palace and transferred her and her servants to the harem's best quarters.

Esther did not reveal her ethnicity or her family background, because Mordecai had ordered her not to make them known. Every day Mordecai took a walk in front of the harem's courtyard to learn how Esther was doing and to see what was happening to her.

During the year before each young woman's turn to go to King Ahasuerus, the harem regulation required her to receive beauty treatments with oil of myrrh for six months and then with perfumes and cosmetics for another six months. When the young woman would go to the king, she was given whatever she requested to take with her from the harem to the palace. She would go in the evening, and in the morning she would return to a second harem under the supervision of the king's eunuch Shaashgaz, keeper of the concubines. She never went to the king again, unless he desired her and summoned her by name.

(ESTHER 2:1–14)

Though **FREQUENTLY RECOGNIZED AS BRAVE** and faithful, Esther is not often regarded as a woman of hospitality. However, she is a recipient of great hospitality. When the king began his search for a new queen, his advisors suggested collecting the most beautiful young women in the kingdom and giving them extensive beauty treatments before the king chose one for his queen. As an attractive young virgin, Esther was taken into the king's court, subjected to palace life whether she wanted it or not.

Hegai, the eunuch in charge of the harem, took to Esther quickly and showed her great favor. We don't know how Hegai felt about his situation, but we know he gave Esther what he could. He extended incredible hospitality to this young, secretly Jewish woman, and offered her what he was able to, namely, special beauty treatments and food that he likely assumed would help her chances to become queen. He also showed her kindness and favor by giving her seven female attendants from the royal household and moving her to the best room in the palace.

Living in the king's court was not something Esther had chosen—it kept her from having a life of her own. In addition to living in unfamiliar quarters with people she didn't know and expectations she didn't understand, she was hiding the dangerous secret of her Jewish heritage. If she'd been wary of Hegai's hospitality or unwilling to accept his kindness, it would have been understandable. Thankfully, Esther took a leap of faith and welcomed his help. Hegai's hospitality was a comfort to her in a difficult time.

> **LIKE ESTHER, OUR LIVES CAN CHANGE IN UNEXPECTED WAYS WHEN WE ARE BRAVE ENOUGH TO ACCEPT THE GIFT OF HOSPITALITY.**

Sometimes we are called to be generous hosts, opening our homes and our lives to bless others. But other times, we are the ones being offered hospitality. In those cases we have a choice: to spurn a kind gesture out of fear or to receive it graciously with discernment. We can be greatly blessed by relationships that grow out of hospitality, and God can use them to fulfill His plans for our lives. Like Esther, our lives can change in unexpected ways when we are brave enough to accept the gift of hospitality.

The Lord knew what would move the king to choose Esther as queen, ensuring that she could one day be in a position to save her people. So God used Hegai's hospitality, favor, and kindness to help guide her through the process.

His hospitality gave way to becoming a valued advisor, and Esther accepted his counsel, which would eventually land her in the position God had for her all along. The Lord's hand was firmly on Esther's life, and Hegai's hospitality was evidence to Esther of the Lord's favor.

Hegai likely did not know the full effect his generous hospitality had on Esther, but the Lord used all of his efforts to bless a frightened young woman in a new world who would one day save the entire Jewish community from being killed. And if the Jews had been killed, Christ never would have been born into it! In so many ways Hegai's hospitality, and Esther's acceptance of it, preserved the line of Jesus as well as our salvation.

Prayer

Dear God, thank You for being with me, no matter where I go. Thank You for protecting me and guiding me, no matter how strange my surroundings seem to me. I know You see all and know all; I know You love me and have good plans for me. Thank You, God. And please help me see the ways You're working in my life. Help me recognize the paths I should take and the friendships I should pursue. Please show me who to trust and what to do. Help me receive the warm hospitality of others, like Esther did, even if it comes through a person I don't expect. Remind me that I have no idea what a small act of hospitality might do for someone else's life or even salvation. I love You, Lord. Amen.

DAY 30

Rebekah

"LORD, God of my master Abraham," he prayed, "make this happen for me today, and show kindness to my master Abraham. I am standing here at the spring where the daughters of the men of the town are coming out to draw water. Let the girl to whom I say, 'Please lower your water jug so that I may drink,' and who responds, 'Drink, and I'll water your camels also'—let her be the one you have appointed for your servant Isaac. By this I will know that you have shown kindness to my master."

Before he had finished speaking, there was Rebekah—daughter of Bethuel son of Milcah, the wife of Abraham's brother Nahor—coming with a jug on her shoulder. Now the girl was very beautiful, a virgin—no man had been intimate with her. She went down to the spring, filled her jug, and came up. Then the servant ran to meet her and said, "Please let me have a little water from your jug."

She replied, "Drink, my lord." She quickly lowered her jug to her hand and gave him a drink. When she had finished giving him a drink, she said, "I'll also draw water for your camels until they have had enough to drink." She quickly emptied her jug into the trough and hurried to the well again to draw water. She drew water for all his camels while the man silently watched her to see whether or not the LORD had made his journey a success.

As the camels finished drinking, the man took a gold ring weighing half a shekel, and for her wrists two bracelets weighing ten shekels of gold. "Whose daughter are you?" he asked. "Please tell me, is there room in your father's house for us to spend the night?"

She answered him, "I am the daughter of Bethuel son of Milcah, whom she bore to Nahor." She also said to him, "We have plenty of straw and feed and a place to spend the night."

Then the man knelt low, worshiped the LORD, and said, "Blessed be the LORD, the God of my master Abraham, who has not withheld his kindness and faithfulness from my master. As for me, the LORD has led me on the journey to the house of my master's relatives."

(GENESIS 24:12–27)

Before SHE BECAME THE MOTHER of Israel, Rebekah was a simple woman living in Nahor. Abraham sent his servant to find a wife among his family's people. His servant specifically asked God for a sign of hospitality from a woman in order to know which woman to choose as Isaac's wife. Without knowing any of that, Rebekah was kind and generous, proving to Abraham's servant that she would make a fine wife for Isaac. She showed incredible hospitality to Abraham's servant, giving him a drink from the well, watering his camels, and inviting him to stay with her family.

Abraham's servant was concerned about finding the right wife for his master's son, and he was unsure how he would even find one option. He'd been given some strict parameters for this wife-finding expedition, and he was nervous. *What if I can't locate Abraham's family? What if I can't find a woman willing to travel so far? What if her family doesn't trust me? What if I can't find someone good enough?* Rebekah's kindness was a specific answer to prayer—not just that Isaac would have a good wife, but also that the servant would be able to complete Abraham's mission successfully.

Abraham's servant did not have reason to worry as he did. God was guiding him the entire time, leading him straight to the woman He had chosen for Isaac. And Rebekah was lovely inside and out, just as kind as she was beautiful. When the servant picked her out of the crowd to ask for water, she didn't hesitate. She offered him water and then, going above and beyond, offered to get water for his camels as well. When he boldly asked if her father had room for guests, she eagerly offered their home. And when he finally revealed the reason for his visit, explaining that she would have to leave her home and travel a great distance to meet and marry Isaac, she agreed. And as we learn in Genesis 24:67, Isaac indeed loved her deeply. More than that, we know that their children's lineage eventually led to the coming of Christ!

> REBEKAH'S HOSPITALITY WAS EXACTLY THE KINDNESS ABRAHAM'S SERVANT NEEDED, AND IMPACTED THE COURSE OF SALVATION HISTORY.

Do you ever get "weird" ideas that pop up out of nowhere? Or feel a "random" nudge—to offer help, to share an encouraging word or meal, to invite someone you just met into your event, your home, your life? What if those nudges aren't actually out of nowhere? What if they're prompts from God, preparing you to meet someone's needs, to be the answer to his or her prayers? What if, by obeying God and offering kindness, you are in turn as blessed as the one you bless?

While it's not always easy, hospitality is an incredible gift that God's people can gladly and easily give one another, whether it is as simple as a drink of water or a place to stay the night. Rebekah's hospitality was exactly the kindness Abraham's servant needed, and like so many other stories in the Bible, it was yet another way God was preserving the line of Christ unbeknownst to the people involved. Sometimes what seem like the smallest acts of hospitality are incredible gifts to those who receive them, and even impact the course of salvation history.

Prayer

Dear God, thank You for stories like this one, where we can see You moving all the parts together and writing one amazing story! Thank You for using each one of us to fulfill Your plans. And thank You for including me in Your plans. God, please help me pay attention when You nudge me. Help me take action when You ask me to, and to do it willingly with a happy heart. I know You can use everything we do and everything we are, Lord, so I ask that You use me. Use everything I have, everything I can do to reach people for You. I want to be a good host, a good neighbor, a good friend. Please protect me from laziness, from busyness, from apathy, from ignorance. Open my eyes and my heart, and keep them open. Give me the opportunity to offer hospitality, like I see in the life of Rebekah, and use me to answer prayers or even bring salvation to someone. Thank You, Lord. I love You and want to show others that love. Amen.

The Widow of Zarephath

*Then the word of the L*ORD *came to him: "Get up, go to Zarephath that belongs to Sidon and stay there. Look, I have commanded a woman who is a widow to provide for you there." So Elijah got up and went to Zarephath. When he arrived at the city gate, there was a widow gathering wood. Elijah called to her and said, "Please bring me a little water in a cup and let me drink." As she went to get it, he called to her and said, "Please bring me a piece of bread in your hand."*

*But she said, "As the L*ORD *your God lives, I don't have anything baked—only a handful of flour in the jar and a bit of oil in the jug. Just now, I am gathering a couple of sticks in order to go prepare it for myself and my son so we can eat it and die."*

*Then Elijah said to her, "Don't be afraid; go and do as you have said. But first make me a small loaf from it and bring it out to me. Afterward, you may make some for yourself and your son, for this is what the L*ORD *God of Israel says, 'The flour jar will not become empty and the oil jug will not run dry until the day the L*ORD *sends rain on the surface of the land.'"*

*So she proceeded to do according to the word of Elijah. Then the woman, Elijah, and her household ate for many days. The flour jar did not become empty, and the oil jug did not run dry, according to the word of the L*ORD *he had spoken through Elijah.*

After this, the son of the woman who owned the house became ill. His illness got worse until he stopped breathing. She said to Elijah, "Man of God, why are you here? Have you come to call attention to my iniquity so that my son is put to death?"

*But Elijah said to her, "Give me your son." So he took him from her arms, brought him up to the upstairs room where he was staying, and laid him on his own bed. Then he cried out to the L*ORD *and said, "L*ORD *my God, have you also brought tragedy on the widow I am staying with by killing her son?" Then he stretched himself out over the boy three times. He cried out to the L*ORD *and said, "L*ORD *my God, please let this boy's life come into him again!"*

*So the L*ORD *listened to Elijah, and the boy's life came into him again, and he lived. Then Elijah took the boy, brought him down from the upstairs room into the house, and gave him to his mother. Elijah said, "Look, your son is alive."*

*Then the woman said to Elijah, "Now I know you are a man of God and the L*ORD*'s word from your mouth is true."*

(1 KINGS 17:8–24)

Hospitality CAN BE STRESSFUL. HOSTING other people in your home, hoping they feel warm and full when they leave, can put strain on any family but especially one that doesn't have enough in the first place. It's easy to share food and space and life when you have an abundance. But when the fridge is bare, it's still a few days from payday, and an unexpected guest asks for a snack, sharing is a little more difficult. This is what the widow of Zarephath learned.

The woman Elijah met at the gate of Sidon had nothing. She and her son were starving, and she had nothing to give the two of them, let alone anyone else. When Elijah asked her for water and bread, she turned him down. But when Elijah insisted, claiming there would be enough, she shared with him what little she had. She gave it without conditions, but God returned her gift exponentially when her son later became sick. The very prophet she'd built a relationship with and sacrificially served would be the same man who prayed to God when her son died and brought him back to life.

How can you offer sacrificial hospitality? Who can you invite into your home and your life, despite the inconvenience or discomfort their addition might cause? Will you give and serve even when you're tired? When your house is too small? When your guest room only holds a lumpy, hand-me-down couch? When you are booked solid from morning to night? When you have too much month left at the end of your dollar? Ask God to help you become a gracious host, even when you have nothing left to give—and He will. He always does.

> THE WIDOW'S HOSPITALITY WAS A GRACIOUS GIFT TO ELIJAH, EVEN THOUGH SHE HAD ALMOST NOTHING TO GIVE.

Hospitality often demands a lot. But God is always faithful to provide for the needs of His people when He asks them to give to others. God provided for the woman and her son, and for Elijah. The small jug of oil and jar of flour did not run out until more rain came on the land. They had exactly what they needed. The widow's hospitality was a gracious gift to Elijah, even though she had almost nothing to give. Hospitality does not often mean extravagance, but sharing and giving out of the resources God has provided, no matter how little or how plentiful.

Prayer

God, thank You for everything You've given me. I know that everything I have is Yours, that every good gift comes from You—so I thank You. Thank You for the best gift of all: my salvation. I want to be a good steward of all the blessings You've given me, Lord. Please help me be generous. Show me who I can serve, who I can invite in, who I can welcome. Help me share what I have, even when it makes me nervous or takes more than I want to give. Help me trust You to provide for my every need, to give me everything I need to be a good neighbor and friend and host. Thank You, God. Thank You for using me to love Your children, and thank You for giving us everything we need. Amen.

WOMEN *of* GRATITUDE

DAY 32

Miriam

When Pharaoh's horses with his chariots and horsemen went into the sea, the LORD brought the water of the sea back over them. But the Israelites walked through the sea on dry ground. Then the prophetess Miriam, Aaron's sister, took a tambourine in her hand, and all the women came out following her with tambourines and dancing. Miriam sang to them:

Sing to the LORD,
for he is highly exalted;
he has thrown the horse
and its rider into the sea.

Then Moses led Israel on from the Red Sea, and they went out to the Wilderness of Shur. They journeyed for three days in the wilderness without finding water. They came to Marah, but they could not drink the water at Marah because it was bitter—that is why it was named Marah.

The people grumbled to Moses, "What are we going to drink?" So he cried out to the LORD, and the LORD showed him a tree. When he threw it into the water, the water became drinkable.

The LORD made a statute and ordinance for them at Marah, and he tested them there. He said, "If you will carefully obey the LORD your God, do what is right in his sight, pay attention to his commands, and keep all his statutes, I will not inflict any illnesses on you that I inflicted on the Egyptians. For I am the LORD who heals you."

Then they came to Elim, where there were twelve springs and seventy date palms, and they camped there by the water.

(EXODUS 15:19–27)

Miriam **AND THE REST OF** the Israelites had already endured so much when they experienced the plagues of Egypt. God saved them from destruction and then from the wrath of the Egyptians at the Red Sea. But instead of pressing on through the desert the moment they crossed the sea, the Israelites stopped to praise the Lord for what He had done for them. Moses, Miriam's brother, sang a song of praise. Then Miriam picked up a tambourine and led all the women of Israel in dancing and singing.

In that moment when the waters rushed back together, covering the Egyptians and saving the Israelites, only God knew that this was just the beginning of their journey. Moses, Aaron, and Miriam were following God's leading one day at a time; they had no idea how long they'd be wandering in the desert, seeking God and His promised land. But without realizing that their choices on that day could set a standard for years to come, Moses and Miriam chose to stop their journey and thank God for all He'd done so far. They chose to worship right away, not waiting for a more convenient time or a more comfortable place. They showed the Israelites by their example that worship and gratitude was a priority.

> **MOSES AND MIRIAM CHOSE TO STOP THEIR JOURNEY AND THANK GOD FOR ALL HE'D DONE SO FAR.**

Overwhelmed with thanksgiving and perhaps inspired by her brother's worship, Miriam led the women, praising God and singing, "Sing to the Lord, for he is highly exalted." She refused to let the moment pass without praising God for what He had done. His work was magnificent and deserved praise. And by stopping to praise God, Miriam created a precedent in Israel and a lasting memory for the people. When they faced difficulty and doubt in the future, they would be able to look back on that day, remember what God had done, and trust His faithfulness.

Any doubt about the importance of putting worship first was erased just a few days later. Faced with great thirst from walking through the desert and water that wasn't fit to drink, the Israelites began to complain. How quickly we forget! The Lord had just rescued them from a vicious king who'd enslaved them for years. He had just split open the sea to give them safe passage and then swallowed up the army that followed to capture them. And in the span of less than a week, the Israelites went from thanking God for His provision to whining about their thirst.

Rather than despair of how quick the Israelites were to change their tune at the first new sign of trouble, we can learn from Miriam's forethought and intentional gratitude. She may not have known how many years of struggle they would face, but she knew they were walking into the wilderness. She probably knew that short or lengthy, their journey would be a hard one and the Israelites would need an anchor to help them recover their thankfulness for God's faithful work in their lives. What better way to help them remember than a celebration of God's goodness, complete with singing and dancing and praising Him for what He had done until now?

When our days are full and our lives are busy, it can be easy to move quickly from one challenge to the next. After all, at times it feels like as soon as one problem is solved, another one pops up. Who has time to pause and reflect, to stop and pray? We do.

No matter what trials God has taken us through, we cannot deny His hand in our rescue. We cannot ignore that regardless of our own efforts, we would still be fighting and running and panicking if He hadn't come through with a supernatural solution. And when He does step in and intervene for us, our next step can only be praising Him! When we recognize His provision and His great love for us, we must express our gratitude. If we wait, instead, for a more convenient time or a more comfortable place, we might never get around to it. And if we don't make a habit of thanking God for His work in our lives, we might just end up like the Israelites, whining about bitter water and wandering the wilderness for decades.

Prayer

Heavenly Father, thank You! Thank You for every single thing You do for me—for loving me, for forgiving me, for saving me from myself and from temptation! Thank You for providing every single thing I need, for being with me when life is hard, for promising that someday You will wipe my every tear. Thank You! And God, please forgive me when I forget to be grateful. Forgive me when all I can see is what I lack, not what I have. Remind me that every good gift is from You and that You will give me exactly what I need each day, exactly when I need it. Lord, I sing to You because You are highly exalted. You have done such wondrous works—for the people of Israel, for us all through Christ on the cross, and even in small ways in my everyday life. You are amazing and I'm so grateful You love me. I love You, too. Amen.

Simon's Mother-in-Law

As [Jesus] passed alongside the Sea of Galilee, he saw Simon and Andrew, Simon's brother, casting a net into the sea—for they were fishermen. "Follow me," Jesus told them, "and I will make you fish for people." Immediately they left their nets and followed him. Going on a little farther, he saw James the son of Zebedee and his brother John in a boat putting their nets in order. Immediately he called them, and they left their father Zebedee in the boat with the hired men and followed him.

They went into Capernaum, and right away he entered the synagogue on the Sabbath and began to teach. They were astonished at his teaching because he was teaching them as one who had authority, and not like the scribes.

Just then a man with an unclean spirit was in their synagogue. He cried out, "What do you have to do with us, Jesus of Nazareth? Have you come to destroy us? I know who you are—the Holy One of God!"

Jesus rebuked him saying, "Be silent, and come out of him!" And the unclean spirit threw him into convulsions, shouted with a loud voice, and came out of him.

They were all amazed, and so they began to ask each other: "What is this? A new teaching with authority! He commands even the unclean spirits, and they obey him." At once the news about him spread throughout the entire vicinity of Galilee.

As soon as they left the synagogue, they went into Simon and Andrew's house with James and John. Simon's mother-in-law was lying in bed with a fever, and they told him about her at once. So he went to her, took her by the hand, and raised her up. The fever left her, and she began to serve them.

When evening came, after the sun had set, they brought to him all those who were sick and demon-possessed. The whole town was assembled at the door, and he healed many who were sick with various diseases and drove out many demons. And he would not permit the demons to speak, because they knew him.

(MARK 1:16–34)

When JESUS MET SIMON AND Andrew, His invitation for them to become fishers of men was so compelling that they immediately followed. Their next move was to go into the temple with Jesus. There they witnessed Him teaching with authority, healing, and commanding unclean spirits to leave. Clearly they had made the right decision when they chose to follow this man! It made sense, then, to invite Him to their home.

When the men arrived at Simon and Andrew's house, they found Simon's mother-in-law sick in bed. We're not told how sick she was, and that's okay. God wants all of our concerns laid at His feet, big or small, urgent or not. Likewise, the new disciples told Jesus right away about Simon's mother-in-law. After having just watched Him demonstrate His authority at temple, they were confident Jesus would do something to help her. And He did!

Demonstrating His great compassion and care for those who were hurting, Jesus healed her as she lay ill. He raised her up and her fever left right away. While her words may not be recorded, her actions showed her gratitude to the Savior. Unlike most recovering from a fever, she was not left weak. Rather she was strengthened by the touch of Jesus—and immediately got up and began to serve Jesus and His disciples. She had not expected this type of guest in her home, especially one capable of miracles and healing. But without hesitation she went to work, welcoming Him and thanking Him for what He did for her. And because He was cared for by her, He was prepared to receive the immense number of sick and possessed souls who came for His help later that day.

What has Jesus done for you, friend? Has He healed you, physically or spiritually? Has He rescued you from temptation, from circumstances, from a pit you could not otherwise have escaped? Has He spoken into your heart, and raised you up when you were downcast? Though we may not expect Him to love us and help us, He will and He does.

> **WITHOUT HESITATION SHE WENT TO WORK, WELCOMING JESUS AND THANKING HIM FOR WHAT HE DID FOR HER.**

The same Christ who teaches with utmost authority and commands spirits has compassion for our afflictions and our struggles. Even if we don't feel worthy or have lost hope, He has not forgotten us and will arrive in His perfect timing with His healing touch. And then out of the overflow of our thankful hearts, we must express our gratitude and honor the work of God in our lives.

The response of Simon's mother-in-law revealed her thankfulness. She served the Lord out of the gratitude in her heart for what He had done. He had reached His hand into her life, impacted her personally, and her thankfulness overflowed through her actions. She served because Jesus had healed her. He had blessed her and she wanted to bless Him in return. Gratitude, no matter how it is expressed, always blesses the Lord. Whether it is through words or song or service, gratitude to the Lord always blesses Him.

Prayer

Oh Lord, thank You! Thank You for remembering me and for loving me! I had no idea You would answer my cries for help today, but I can't imagine a better surprise. Thank You for healing me and strengthening me; thank You for caring about what happens to me. God, I am so grateful I can barely contain myself. How can I show You my gratitude? Lord, please help me find a way to show You just how thankful I am. How can I serve You? Who can I tell about You? Guide me, Lord. You blessed me; I want to bless You. Please show me how I can do that, and give me the strength to do it. Thank You, God. Thank You for everything You've done for me. I love You. Amen.

WOMEN *of* SECOND CHANCES

Rachel

When Rachel saw that she was not bearing Jacob any children, she envied her sister. "Give me sons, or I will die!" she said to Jacob.

Jacob became angry with Rachel and said, "Am I in God's place, who has withheld offspring from you?"

Then she said, "Here is my maid Bilhah. Go sleep with her, and she'll bear children for me so that through her I too can build a family." So Rachel gave her slave Bilhah to Jacob as a wife, and he slept with her. Bilhah conceived and bore Jacob a son. Rachel said, "God has vindicated me; yes, he has heard me and given me a son," so she named him Dan.

Rachel's slave Bilhah conceived again and bore Jacob a second son. Rachel said, "In my wrestlings with God, I have wrestled with my sister and won," and she named him Naphtali.

(GENESIS 30:1–8)

We've **HEARD THE STORY OF** the sisters, Leah and Rachel. We've heard how their father tricked Jacob by replacing the bride he wanted (Rachel) with the one he did not (Leah). And most often we've talked about how hardworking and faithful Jacob was, and how neglected and mistreated Leah was. But rarely do we remember the other main player in this story.

Shapely and beautiful, Rachel was the favored daughter and the sought-after bride. But though Jacob loved her and asked for her hand in marriage, Rachel had to wait seven long years, watching while her sister Leah took the wifely role she desperately wanted in his life. When she finally was allowed to marry Jacob, Rachel found herself trapped in the worst kind of competition: competition with family. She was in constant competition with her sister, Leah, over the number of children they had and which sister had the love of their husband.

Though she was loved by Jacob, Rachel was barren and desperate to have a child. Her infertility led to tension between her and her husband, on top of the already complicated relationship she had with her sister. And it even led to her plan of offering Jacob her servant as a means to provide a surrogate mother, settling for something less than God's plan in her desperation for children. But God did not abandon her—not when she waited for marriage, and not when she waited for pregnancy.

*Then God remembered Rachel. He listened to her and opened her womb.
She conceived and bore a son, and she said, "God has taken away my
disgrace." She named him Joseph and said, "May the L*ORD* add another son to
me." (Gen. 30:22–24)*

God remembered Rachel, and allowed her to conceive and give birth to a son.
Finally she would see her dreams come true. She would bear a son with her
husband; all was finally right in her life. But rather than take credit for this turn
of events or further hurting her sister with the news, Rachel realized she wasn't
responsible for her fortune or her future. She recognized that the son she bore
was from God, and she stopped to give thanks to Him. She understood what
God had done for her, by taking away the disgrace she bore when she was
childless.

God was faithful to remember Rachel, and Rachel was faithful to remember the
Lord. She honored Him after the birth of her son. Her thankfulness no doubt
impacted her attitude, and allowed her to cling to the goodness of God instead
of competing with her sister. By focusing on what God had given her instead of
what others had, Rachel was able to fully
rejoice and experience gratitude for the
beautiful gift she had received.

> BY FOCUSING ON
> WHAT GOD HAD GIVEN
> HER INSTEAD OF
> WHAT OTHERS HAD,
> RACHEL WAS ABLE
> TO FULLY REJOICE
> AND EXPERIENCE
> GRATITUDE.

Does life feel unfair right now? Have
you gotten the short end of the stick,
the blame for something that was out
of your control, the leftovers or even a
loss while others seem to be blessed
over and over? Does that make you feel
like lashing out at those who love you
most? Stop. Wait—on the Lord and on
your temper to cool. Remember what
God has promised. Remember that He
has vowed to never leave you, to work all things together for your good and His
glory, to remember you and bless you with everything you need. Remember!

Sometimes it's so tempting to try and get ahead of God, or force His hand in a
situation. We know His promises and we've heard His call, and we just want to
make all the good stuff happen right now. In all sorts of ways and circumstances,
we look for a "surrogate" opportunity instead of waiting on God's timing and
plan. Surely Rachel felt crushing impatience, along with disappointment and
even jealousy, when nothing in her life turned out the way she'd imagined and
hoped and believed it would. But even after she took matters into her own

hands, even after she raged against her husband, her sister, and possibly even her God, the Lord did not forget her or leave her alone. Though she didn't wait on him the first time around, He gave her a second chance and blessed her abundantly, in His time and His ways.

May we be more patient than Rachel when faced with another wait, another letdown, another gaping silence. May we love our families and friends even when their lives seem more blessed than ours, even when they seem to be the ones holding us back. And may we prepare our hearts for the day God remembers us, so we are ready to shout praise and thanksgiving for all He has given us. May we replace resentment with gratitude and bitterness with faithful anticipation for the Lord. May we avoid creating our own surrogate strategies, and trust in God's plan instead.

Prayer

Heavenly Father, thank You for Your patience. Thank You for loving me even when I lash out, when I don't listen, when I'm less than loving. Forgive me, please, for being jealous and bitter when other people's lives look like the one I wanted, when they get the things I've begged You for. Help me remember that Your plans and Your timing are good—so much better than mine! And God, when the time comes that I get a glimpse of Your plan, when Your will comes to fruition, please help me remember You. Help me remember that all good gifts come from You, that You never left my side when I was brokenhearted, that all of this is for Your glory and not just my good! Thank You, God, for loving me through seasons of little and seasons of plenty. Thank You for showing me how blessed I am through it all. Thank You for offering me second chances when I fail to wait on You, and teach me to trust in Your plans instead of my own Thank You for everything You're going to do in me and through me. Thank You. Amen.

Eve

Now the serpent was the most cunning of all the wild animals that the LORD God had made. He said to the woman, "Did God really say, 'You can't eat from any tree in the garden'?"

The woman said to the serpent, "We may eat the fruit from the trees in the garden. But about the fruit of the tree in the middle of the garden, God said, 'You must not eat it or touch it, or you will die.'"

"No! You will not die," the serpent said to the woman. "In fact, God knows that when you eat it your eyes will be opened and you will be like God, knowing good and evil." The woman saw that the tree was good for food and delightful to look at, and that it was desirable for obtaining wisdom. So she took some of its fruit and ate it; she also gave some to her husband, who was with her, and he ate it. Then the eyes of both of them were opened, and they knew they were naked; so they sewed fig leaves together and made coverings for themselves.

Then the man and his wife heard the sound of the LORD God walking in the garden at the time of the evening breeze, and they hid from the LORD God among the trees of the garden. So the LORD God called out to the man and said to him, "Where are you?"

And he said, "I heard you in the garden, and I was afraid because I was naked, so I hid."

Then he asked, "Who told you that you were naked? Did you eat from the tree that I commanded you not to eat from?"

The man replied, "The woman you gave to be with me—she gave me some fruit from the tree, and I ate."

So the LORD God asked the woman, "What is this you have done?"

And the woman said, "The serpent deceived me, and I ate."...

The man named his wife Eve because she was the mother of all the living. The Lord God made clothing from skins for the man and his wife, and he clothed them.

The LORD God said, "Since the man has become like one of us, knowing good and evil, he must not reach out, take from the tree of life, eat, and live forever." So the Lord God sent him away from the garden of Eden to work the ground from which he was taken. He drove the man out and stationed the cherubim and the flaming, whirling sword east of the garden of Eden to guard the way to the tree of life.

(GENESIS 3:1–13, 20–24)

Has **ANY WOMAN BEEN BLAMED** for more than Eve? The fall of mankind literally rests on her shoulders, no thanks to the serpent who deceived her, or her husband who did not intervene when she was being tempted. Eve certainly could not comprehend the way a single choice she'd made in a fog of confusion and pride would affect all people for all time. After all, in the beginning "all people" only included Adam and Eve. They were it, so consequences so far-reaching would have been unfathomable. Yet, that's all the more reason she should have trusted God. And while she couldn't imagine what one choice would lead to, she didn't have to imagine what it was like to commune with God, face to face, every day. She and Adam had been given that privilege along with the freedom to do pretty much everything except eat from one tree. In one way Eve lacked perspective but in another, she had it in spades.

The first mistake in history also led to the greatest second chance and promise of redemption. Eve had broken God's law, doing the one thing He asked her not to do. She craved wisdom, and believed God was withholding from her. But He didn't leave her in her brokenness.

While there were consequences for her actions, God gave her a second chance. He promised to redeem her and make her the mother of all the living. He granted her and her husband the greatest responsibility, of populating the earth. He promised that one day, a Savior from her bloodline would crush the serpent and destroy his hold on man. God not only gave Eve a second chance, but He promised to fully and completely redeem her life and all of mankind through her offspring. He fulfilled His promise to her, bringing about redemption and grace through her second chance.

> GOD BOUGHT ABOUT REDEMPTION AND GRACE THROUGH EVE'S SECOND CHANCE.

Are you feeling burdened by sin today? Like Eve, do you see the way it has affected others in ways you didn't predict or understand? Take heart in God's response to Eve's grievous mistake. Though she had to face consequences for her sin, He did not completely turn His back on her. You may face the natural fallout for your sin; that is the way the world works. But God won't make you face them alone. He will be with you. And He won't leave you in a pit of regret and despair, either. Because the Savior really did come in the man of Jesus Christ, God has erased your sin and made you white as snow. The cross has taken care of the penalty for the ways you've harmed yourself and others, and

God will redeem your life with His good plans. No matter what you've done, no matter how far you've fallen, God loves you and He will not leave you.

Prayer

Oh God, I've messed up. I've made a mistake so big I'm not sure I can recover. I know You will forgive me if I ask . . . so I'm asking. Please forgive me, Lord. Forgive me my pride and my selfishness. Forgive me and heal the wounds I've created. Be with me as I wade through all the consequences I'm facing, God. Keep me focused on You; don't let me get sucked into the mud again. I know this pain won't last forever, but right now it feels unending. Give me Your strength, God; give me peace even when everything around me is falling apart. And thank You for the cross, the work of Christ that has paid the price for this sin I've committed. Thank You that the cross does not leave us separated from You as Adam and Eve were; thank You that it gives us all a second chance to draw near to You instead. Thank You, God. Thank You for forgiving me and saving me from myself. Thank You. I love You. Amen.

Woman Caught in Adultery

At dawn [Jesus] went to the temple again, and all the people were coming to him. He sat down and began to teach them.

Then the scribes and the Pharisees brought a woman caught in adultery, making her stand in the center. "Teacher," they said to him, "this woman was caught in the act of committing adultery. In the law Moses commanded us to stone such women. So what do you say?" They asked this to trap him, in order that they might have evidence to accuse him.

Jesus stooped down and started writing on the ground with his finger. When they persisted in questioning him, he stood up and said to them, "The one without sin among you should be the first to throw a stone at her." Then he stooped down again and continued writing on the ground. When they heard this, they left one by one, starting with the older men. Only he was left, with the woman in the center. When Jesus stood up, he said to her, "Woman, where are they? Has no one condemned you?"

"No one, Lord," she answered.

"Neither do I condemn you," said Jesus. "Go, and from now on do not sin anymore."

(JOHN 8:2–11)

The **PHARISEES SEEMED TO DELIGHT** in catching people in sin. Most of the time that we see them in Scripture, they are attempting to trick Jesus—including this instance when they caught a woman committing adultery and then used her in their efforts to trap Jesus. Caught in the act of breaking the law, this woman had no defense and no defender. Thrown into a crowd of men, possibly in a state of undress, she was completely defenseless.

Until the moment her path crossed Jesus', that is. At that moment she was given an advocate, someone to offer her protection from the lethal consequences of her actions. Though she was saved from the stoning, Jesus didn't turn a blind eye to her sin. He forgave her, yes, but then commissioned her into a life that looked different, a life free from sin.

This woman had every reason to be stoned to death like the law commanded. But Jesus had come to fulfill the law, not enforce it, so that those under it could rest in His record instead of their own. He granted the woman caught in adultery, along with the rest of humanity, a second chance. With her second chance, Jesus did not say, "You're forgiven, go do whatever you want." He did not condemn her, but He did command her to abandon a life of sin.

The woman caught in adultery learned that a relationship with Jesus is not a "get out of hell free" card. Forgiveness is not permission to live however one wants, with an understanding that Jesus will make it all right in the end. Instead, it's an invitation to live a life full of love and light and righteousness, designed to point others to God. He didn't rescue her from a physical death only to return her to a spiritual one. No, Jesus redirected her path toward holiness, toward wholeness.

This encounter between Jesus and the woman caught in adultery was actually just one more attempt by the Pharisees to trick Jesus into sinning. They plotted against Him, looking for any opening to prove He was not who He said He was. Surely this woman's situation would do it!

But, no. Jesus refused to allow the religious officials to use the woman to condemn Him—or to use Him to condemn her. Rather, He raised the questions of sin and innocence, since the Pharisees were acting on their assumptions of both. Turning down their invitation to judge her and therefore sentencing her to death, He bent over and began writing in the dirt.

> WHEN JESUS GAVE THE WOMAN CAUGHT IN ADULTERY A SECOND CHANCE, HE DIDN'T DO IT TO GIVE HER FREEDOM *TO* SIN, BUT INSTEAD FREEDOM *FROM* IT.

Nobody knows what He wrote that day. But whatever it was, it caused the Pharisees to rethink their plan. Jesus declined the offer to serve as the woman's judge and jury and returned that responsibility to the Pharisees. But He attached a condition to their judgment; He said that whoever had not sinned himself should be the one to punish her. Strangely enough, nobody volunteered and the woman was left alone.

Do you feel exposed? Do you worry that someone is plotting your punishment, waiting for you to mess up? Have you already been judged and found guilty? Friend, you are not alone and this is not the end. Though it may seem like you are without an excuse and without defense—your only options being penance or escaping back to the darkness—that's not the case. Just like He did for the woman caught in the act of adultery, Jesus will rescue you—from your sin and from the judgment it demands. His death and resurrection has already paid the price for the mistakes you have made and the ones you are making right now. And if you trust in that, He will lift you out of the darkness and point you toward the light. He will rescue you for a reason: a second chance.

When Jesus gave the woman caught in adultery a second chance, He didn't do it to give her freedom *to* sin, but instead freedom *from* it. He did it to show her that her life was worth living well and that she had the power to choose that path instead. That's exactly what He offers us today, and that is a second chance worth taking.

Prayer

Oh, Lord, I don't want You to look at me. I don't want anyone to look at me—to look at me and see what I've done, who I've become. I don't know why I've done these things, but I've been doing them long enough that I don't know anything else. I don't know who I am without these things. It's no wonder I'm facing the consequences of my choices now; I don't deserve anything better. But . . . but You say that You love me anyway. Is that true? You say that You came to save the world, not to condemn it. Could that apply to me? Is it possible? Jesus, save me. Please. Save me from everyone who is so angry with me, and save me from myself. Thank You for the second chance that You offered to me in the gospel—where You gave me a perfect record to stand on that's not mine. I will take this second chance! I will do things differently since You've freed me from sin. I will. Thank You, God. Thank You for loving me and protecting me and believing in me and forgiving me. Thank You. Amen.

The Mother of Samson

The Israelites again did what was evil in the LORD's sight, so the LORD handed them over to the Philistines forty years. There was a certain man from Zorah, from the family of Dan, whose name was Manoah; his wife was unable to conceive and had no children. The angel of the LORD appeared to the woman and said to her, "It is true that you are unable to conceive and have no children, but you will conceive and give birth to a son. Now please be careful not to drink wine or beer, or to eat anything unclean; for indeed, you will conceive and give birth to a son. You must never cut his hair, because the boy will be a Nazirite to God from birth, and he will begin to save Israel from the power of the Philistines."

Then the woman went and told her husband, "A man of God came to me. He looked like the awe-inspiring angel of God. I didn't ask him where he came from, and he didn't tell me his name. He said to me, 'You will conceive and give birth to a son. Therefore, do not drink wine or beer, and do not eat anything unclean, because the boy will be a Nazirite to God from birth until the day of his death.'"

Manoah prayed to the LORD and said, "Please, Lord, let the man of God you sent come again to us and teach us what we should do for the boy who will be born."

God listened to Manoah, and the angel of God came again to the woman. She was sitting in the field, and her husband Manoah was not with her. The woman ran quickly to her husband and told him, "The man who came to me the other day has just come back!"

So Manoah got up and followed his wife. When he came to the man, he asked, "Are you the man who spoke to my wife?"

"I am," he said.

Then Manoah asked, "When your words come true, what will be the boy's responsibilities and work?"

The angel of the LORD answered Manoah, "Your wife needs to do everything I told her. She must not eat anything that comes from the grapevine or drink wine or beer. And she must not eat anything unclean. Your wife must do everything I have commanded her."

(JUDGES 13:1–14)

The **MOTHER OF SAMSON, THE** wife of Manoah, a childless woman; all of these descriptions give us information about this courageous, unnamed woman. She was known for having no children and being unable to conceive. Then Lord opened her womb. An angel appeared to her and revealed to her that she would have a son, one who would be a Nazirite and set apart to the Lord.

It's remarkable how quickly this woman believed the angel—and how willing she was to follow his orders during her miraculous pregnancy. As soon as the angel spoke about her infertility, she knew he was from God. And when he promised that the long season of being labeled childless was about to come to an end, she didn't question him. She simply believed. After all this time, she would finally be a mother! She didn't even flinch when the angel announced that her son would be a Nazirite, dedicated to serving the Lord while observing strict vows of abstinence and purity. And when instructed to follow those rules during her pregnancy—to prepare her son, perhaps, or to develop in him or in herself strength and obedience—she did so.

> THOUGH SHE HAD LITTLE TO NO VALUE IN THE WORLD'S EYES, GOD GAVE HER A SECOND CHANCE AND REDEEMED HER LIFE.

Other similar stories in the Bible tell of couples given promises of babies after years of infertility. The difference in this story is that Samson's mother and father never once doubted—the angel, each other, God's plan. They didn't question any of it and simply obeyed. Samson's mother was faithful to do all the Lord had asked of her. While much of her life she'd probably believed she had little or no value because of her barrenness, God gave her a second chance and redeemed her life. He gave her a son who would give Israel relief from their enemy, the Philistines, and would judge and lead the people.

So the woman gave birth to a son and named him Samson. The boy grew, and the Lord blessed him. (Judg. 13:24)

Are you afraid that you've missed your last chance? That you're no longer useful to the Lord or this world? Do you wonder if God decided somewhere along the way that you weren't worthy of having a place in His plan? That is not true! Do not give up! No matter what has already happened, no matter what loss or disappointment or silence you've experience until now, your story is not over.

God will use you. And when He does, don't question His timing or His plans. Simply celebrate and follow Him!

While Samson's life does not provide an example to follow, his mother's faithfulness and hope when she was childless is encouraging. Regardless of what she may have believed about her life, God was not finished with her. He had a second chance planned for her and He was only waiting for His perfect timing to bring it about. For her, it was infertility; for you, it may be something else. Regardless of the particulars, know that God gives us chance after chance to be used for His glory; all we must do is watch and wait for the opportunity to come, and follow His lead when it does.

Prayer

Oh Lord, it feels like my life is over. Or maybe it feels like it will never get started. Whatever words I use, the point is that I'm tired of waiting. I'm tired of hoping and crying and hearing only silence and feeling only emptiness. Will You never answer me? I know I'm supposed to wait and hope, preparing for the day You come to me like the angel of the Lord came to Samson's mother. I know that, God, but it's so hard. Will You give me strength? Give me patience? Give me a faith strong enough to endure the wait? I want to wait on You; I want to trust that You're coming and that You haven't forgotten me. Help my unbelief, Lord. Help me wait faithfully, and help me see all the chances You want me to take to be used for Your glory. Amen.

Gomer

The word of the Lord that came to Hosea son of Beeri during the reigns of Uzziah, Jotham, Ahaz, and Hezekiah, kings of Judah, and of Jeroboam son of Jehoash, king of Israel.

When the Lord first spoke to Hosea, he said this to him: "Go and marry a woman of promiscuity, and have children of promiscuity, for the land is committing blatant acts of promiscuity by abandoning the Lord."

So he went and married Gomer daughter of Diblaim, and she conceived and bore him a son.

(HOSEA 1:1–3)

Then the Lord said to me, "Go again; show love to a woman who is loved by another man and is an adulteress, just as the Lord loves the Israelites though they turn to other gods and love raisin cakes."

So I bought her for fifteen shekels of silver and five bushels of barley. I said to her, "You are to live with me many days. You must not be promiscuous or belong to any man, and I will act the same way toward you."

For the Israelites must live many days without king or prince, without sacrifice or sacred pillar, and without ephod or household idols. Afterward, the people of Israel will return and seek the Lord their God and David their king. They will come with awe to the Lord and to his goodness in the last days.

(HOSEA 3)

Gomer **WAS A PROSTITUTE. BUT** her story didn't end there. God redeemed her life, sin and all, to provide a vivid example of love and forgiveness for the Israelites. Hosea, a prophet and her husband, redeemed her from a life of slavery, but Gomer ran from him. She ran back into what she knew, but Hosea came for her and rescued her again. Committed to obeying the incredibly difficult assignment he'd received from God, Hosea loved his wife despite her infidelity and gave her as many second chances as she needed to accept a life of freedom.

Gomer's life of slavery and prostitution may seem foreign to us, but her tendency to return to her sin is sadly familiar. God was using her story as a picture for Israel to understand His love for them. Just like she ran back to her former slavery in the brothel, Israel frequently ran back to their own forms of slavery and idolatry. Just as she trusted in other lovers instead of Hosea, Israel trusted in other nations instead of God.

As much as we shake our heads at both Gomer and Israel, the truth is, we are much like them. Just as they fell back into slavery, disobedience, adultery, and idolatry, we do the same things with God. Every day, we face the temptation to abandon the narrow road to righteousness when following God becomes difficult. But even if we, like Gomer, choose the darkness and pain we've grown accustomed to over His light and love, God does not give up on us. Like Hosea, He pursues us and reaches out to us, offering another chance at redemption.

Hosea was given not just one heavy burden, but two. He was called to marry Gomer, knowing she'd be unfaithful, but that wasn't all. He was also given a harsh message from God for the Israelites; he had the undesirable responsibility to rebuke the children of God, condemning them for their unfaithfulness and predicting destruction and judgment to come.

Because of his personal heartbreak, Hosea was able to clearly communicate God's disappointment and sorrow at the knowledge of Israel's worship of other gods. But because God encouraged him to keep forgiving and rescuing his wife, Hosea was also able to tell the Israelites just how much God loved them, just how high a price He would pay for them, and just how relentless His pursuit of them would be.

> GOD'S LOVE FOR GOMER—LIKE HIS LOVE FOR ISRAEL AND FOR US—WAS ENDLESS.

God's love for Gomer—like His love for the Israelites and for us—was endless. Not only did He send her a faithful man like Hosea to be her husband, but He used Hosea to rescue her from slavery—a man who foreshadowed Christ, the faithful pursuer who would one day not only ask His people to repent from their waywardness, but would also pay for their adultery and idolatry Himself.

God rescued Gomer over and over, blessing her with children and a life of love. And then, even though she struggled to accept these gifts and remain faithful, He used her story to reach the Israelites with the truth of their sin, the judgment they deserved, and His loving forgiveness. Her pain and struggles weren't for naught; God used every single part of her life in His greater plan to rescue the world.

Have you been rescued by God, only to return to your former ways? Was the temptation of the familiar too much to resist? Are you afraid you've blown your chance? It's not too late, friend! You are not too far gone. God loves you with an incomprehensible strength that cannot be stopped merely by our rebellion. He has promised to never abandon us; He has sworn to love us forever. And He will. Even now, as you look longingly at your regrettable but comfortable options, He is reaching for you. He is pursuing you, like a brokenhearted lover, desperate to bring you home and offer you everything He has.

Gomer's experience is a beautiful example of the way God pursues His people and works hard to redeem their lives. Her continued rebellion against Hosea mirrored Israel's rebellion against God. But like Hosea went after Gomer time and time again, God pursues His people despite how many times they fall into sin, so much so that He became a person Himself, to physically come after His people in the person of Jesus. His love is overwhelming, knowing no bounds. He is quick to reach out to His people, giving them second chance after second chance and crafting stories of redemption for each of His children.

Prayer

God . . . are You there? Can You still hear me? Are You still listening? God, I'm so sorry. I'm so sorry I took Your love and Your forgiveness and threw it all away. I'm sorry I walked away from You. I'm sorry I went back and messed up all over again. It's so hard, God. It's so hard to stay away from that life, to walk away for good. Will You help me? Will You still love me? God, I don't take Your forgiveness for granted. I don't. I know the pain You went through to pay for my sin on the cross. I am so grateful that You have given me another chance (and another, and another), and I want to be faithful. I want to learn from Gomer and the Israelites and even my own past. I want to follow You. Please show me how. Amen.

WOMEN *of* BRAVERY

Hannah

There was a man from Ramathaim-zophim in the hill country of Ephraim. His name was Elkanah son of Jeroham, son of Elihu, son of Tohu, son of Zuph, an Ephraimite. He had two wives, the first named Hannah and the second Peninnah. Peninnah had children, but Hannah was childless. This man would go up from his town every year to worship and to sacrifice to the LORD of Armies at Shiloh, where Eli's two sons, Hophni and Phinehas, were the LORD's priests.

Whenever Elkanah offered a sacrifice, he always gave portions of the meat to his wife Peninnah and to each of her sons and daughters. But he gave a double portion to Hannah, for he loved her even though the LORD had kept her from conceiving. Her rival would taunt her severely just to provoke her, because the LORD had kept Hannah from conceiving. Year after year, when she went up to the LORD's house, her rival taunted her in this way. Hannah would weep and would not eat. "Hannah, why are you crying?" her husband Elkanah would ask. "Why won't you eat? Why are you troubled? Am I not better to you than ten sons?"

On one occasion, Hannah got up after they ate and drank at Shiloh. The priest Eli was sitting on a chair by the doorpost of the LORD's temple. Deeply hurt, Hannah prayed to the LORD and wept with many tears. Making a vow, she pleaded, "LORD of Armies, if you will take notice of your servant's affliction, remember and not forget me, and give your servant a son, I will give him to the LORD all the days of his life, and his hair will never be cut."

While she continued praying in the LORD's presence, Eli watched her mouth. Hannah was praying silently, and though her lips were moving, her voice could not be heard. Eli thought she was drunk and said to her, "How long are you going to be drunk? Get rid of your wine!"

"No, my lord," Hannah replied. "I am a woman with a broken heart. I haven't had any wine or beer; I've been pouring out my heart before the LORD. Don't think of me as a wicked woman; I've been praying from the depth of my anguish and resentment."

Eli responded, "Go in peace, and may the God of Israel grant the request you've made of him."

"May your servant find favor with you," she replied. Then Hannah went on her way; she ate and no longer looked despondent.

The next morning Elkanah and Hannah got up early to worship before the LORD. Afterward, they returned home to Ramah. Then Elkanah was intimate with his wife Hannah, and the LORD remembered her. After some time, Hannah conceived and gave birth to a son. She named him Samuel, because she said, "I requested him from the LORD."

(1 SAMUEL 1:1–20)

In A TIME WHEN A woman's worth was equated with her number of children, Hannah had none. She was barren, though loved by her husband. The Lord had closed her womb. Provoked and ridiculed, Hannah endured the shame that came with childlessness for years. Hannah prayed to the Lord, pouring out her heart and her desires to him.

Though she knew asking God for a child could possibly bring her more pain, whether that came in the form of others watching and mocking her futile faith or God simply continuing to say no to her request. But her desire to seek the Lord with her woes outweighed her fear of ridicule or denial. Bravely and faithfully, she came to the Lord with her pain. She ran to Him, knowing He was the only one who could heal her pain and possibly grant her heart's desires. And then, despite her desperate longing for a child, Hannah vowed that, if she were given the chance to bear a son, she would give him back to the Lord.

> **BRAVELY AND FAITHFULLY, HANNAH CAME TO THE LORD WITH HER PAIN.**

Hannah's faithfulness to God despite her pain, along with her recognition that everything belongs to Him, showed great courage. She wanted a son so badly, but she was also deeply committed to God. When her prayers were finally answered and she had a son, she followed through on her commitment. She took him to the temple and said: "I prayed for this boy, and since the LORD gave me what I asked him for, I now give the boy to the LORD. For as long as he lives, he is given to the LORD" (1 Sam. 1:27–28).

What are you longing for? Are you afraid to ask God for your heart's deepest desire? Are you afraid that asking would seem foolish—or that hearing "no" would break your heart even further? Trust God, friend. Trust Him with your heart and your longings. After all, He is the one who created you and your desires, and He is the only one who can fulfill them. He may not answer your prayers according to your expectations or your timing. But when you are faithful to open your heart to Him and take your requests to Him, He will be faithful to hear you and answer you.

Hannah was faithful to bring her requests to the Lord and faithful again to give her son Samuel to the Lord. Her bravery brought Israel the priest who would anoint Israel's first kings and shepherd the nation from the era of judges into the era of kings. May we be as faithful to share our own requests with the Lord; may we be as brave to offer everything we have back to Him.

Prayer

Dear God, I know that You know my every thought, every fear, every longing. I know You created me and know me inside and out. So, Lord, I trust You with my heart. I trust You with the things I wish for most earnestly, the things I want most desperately. Please hear my cries, Lord; search my heart. Am I asking in vain? Is my faith in Your answer futile? Will You answer me? I know Your timing and Your plans are best, God. Please align my heart and my desires with Your will. I ask You for bravery like Hannah's, and I give You everything, Lord. Your will be done. Amen.

DAY 40

Abigail

While David was in the wilderness, he heard that Nabal was shearing sheep, so David sent ten young men instructing them, "Go up to Carmel, and when you come to Nabal, greet him in my name. Then say this: 'Long life to you, and peace to you, peace to your family, and peace to all that is yours. I hear that you are shearing. When your shepherds were with us, we did not harass them, and nothing of theirs was missing the whole time they were in Carmel. Ask your young men, and they will tell you. So let my young men find favor with you, for we have come on a feast day. Please give whatever you have on hand to your servants and to your son David.'"

David's young men went and said all these things to Nabal on David's behalf, and they waited. Nabal asked them, "Who is David? Who is Jesse's son? Many slaves these days are running away from their masters. Am I supposed to take my bread, my water, and my meat that I butchered for my shearers and give them to these men? I don't know where they are from."

David's young men retraced their steps. When they returned to him, they reported all these words. He said to his men, "All of you, put on your swords!" So each man put on his sword, and David also put on his sword. About four hundred men followed David while two hundred stayed with the supplies.

One of Nabal's young men informed Abigail, Nabal's wife: "Look, David sent messengers from the wilderness to greet our master, but he screamed at them. The men treated us very well. When we were in the field, we weren't harassed and nothing of ours was missing the whole time we were living among them. They were a wall around us, both day and night, the entire time we were with them herding the sheep. Now consider carefully what you should do, because there is certain to be trouble for our master and his entire family. He is such a worthless fool nobody can talk to him!"

Abigail hurried, taking two hundred loaves of bread, two clay jars of wine, five butchered sheep, a bushel of roasted grain, one hundred clusters of raisins, and two hundred cakes of pressed figs, and loaded them on donkeys. Then she said to her male servants, "Go ahead of me. I will be right behind you." But she did not tell her husband Nabal.

As she rode the donkey down a mountain pass hidden from view, she saw David and his men coming toward her and met them. David had just said, "I guarded everything that belonged to this man in the wilderness for nothing. He was not missing anything, yet he paid me back evil for good. May God punish me and do so severely if I let any of his males survive until morning.". . .

Then David said to Abigail, "Blessed be the Lord God of Israel, who sent you to meet me today! May your discernment be blessed, and may you be blessed. Today you kept me from participating in bloodshed and avenging myself by my own hand. Otherwise, as surely as the Lord God of Israel lives, who prevented me from harming you, if you had not come quickly to meet me, Nabal wouldn't have had any males left by morning light." Then David accepted what she had brought him and said, "Go home in peace. See, I have heard what you said and have granted your request."

(1 SAMUEL 25:4–22, 32–35)

Abigail **WAS THE WIFE OF** a wicked man, Nabal. He was quick-tempered and foolish and treated everyone harshly. When David's men asked Nabal for provisions, he turned them down, despite the kindness that David's men had shown him. Hearing of this, Abigail took action. She knew her husband was foolish and that David's wrath was coming on her household. She gathered a great many gifts and brought them to David, asking for his forgiveness for her husband's actions.

Not only was Abigail courageous, but she also was wise. When she approached David, bearing provisions and gifts, she knelt in respect and begged his forgiveness. She took responsibility for her husband's offensive response to David's men, noting that she had not been home when they came to ask for help. Her actions made clear the difference between Nabal, selfish and worthless, and herself, intelligent and helpful. She also appealed to David's desire for righteousness by pointing out that by avoiding a battle and bloodshed, his conscience would be clear.

What would you do if those around you insisted on selfish, harmful behavior? What if those in your family or community consistently chose to ignore God's commands, acted in their best interests regardless of consequences, and hurt others on a regular basis? How would you atone for their sins, prevent escalation or retaliation? Would you be bold and stand up for what's right? Would you disregard the opinion of others or even potential threats to your reputation or well-being in order to protect those whom God loves? Would any of us follow Abigail's example of courageous kindness?

> (**ABIGAIL DID WHAT WAS RIGHT REGARDLESS OF THE RISK.**)

Abigail took incredible risks by offering help to David. She risked her husband's wrath by giving away their family's food and supplies, and she risked punishment from David simply by being associated with Nabal. Still, Abigail knew it was up to her to prevent a devastating battle between the two men and so she acted. Rather than fleeing or trying to change her husband's horrible character in just a moment's time, Abigail stepped out in courage and dealt with the problem with her own good and discerning character. She knew that blessing David and his men was the right thing to do, and she did it, without worrying about the repercussions from her foolish husband. Her bravery led her to bless others and save her household, and eventually, become David's wife.

May we be as brave as Abigail, doing what is right regardless of the risk, offering help when others won't, and joining forces with those following God.

Prayer

Dear God,

When I look around I see so many wrongs being committed. I see people behaving badly, concerned only for their own comfort and convenience and determined to ignore the pain or need of others. God, it breaks my heart and it makes me so angry, and I want to help. But I don't know how. I'm not sure what to do, and I'm afraid of what people will say when I do. Will You help me? Will You help me be strong? Will You help me be brave like Abigail, confidently acting with integrity despite the risks? I want to follow You, Lord, even when it's hard. Even when it's scary. Even when it means putting myself right in the middle of a battlefield. Help me, Lord. Grant me protection and courage, and point me in the direction of Your mission for my life. Help me stand strong and stand for You. Help me see when there's an opportunity to walk in when others walk out. Give me the heart to discern when to join forces with someone doing Your will, and help them in a time of need. Draw near to me and help me. Amen.

(in)courage welcomes you

to a place where authentic, brave women
connect deeply with God and others.
Through the power of shared stories and
meaningful resources, (in)courage champions
women and celebrates the strength Jesus gives
to live out our calling as God's daughters.
In the middle of your unfine moments and ordinary days,
you are invited to become a woman of courage.

Join us at **www.incourage.me** and
connect with us on social media!

f 🐦 📷 🅿
@incourage

Looking for your next read?

Check out one of these great books from your friends at

(in)courage

incourage.me/library

The CSB (in)courage Devotional Bible

invites every woman to find her story *within the* greatest story ever told—God's story *of* redemption.

- **312 devotions** by 122 (in)courage community writers
- 10 distinct thematic **reading plans**
- Stories of courage from **50 women** of the Bible
- *and more features!*

Find out more at incourageBible.com

Come on in!

Hospitality is one of the best ways to live out the two greatest commandments: Loving *God* with all your heart and loving your *neighbor* as yourself.

Resources to help you change the world around you, one open door at a time.

Bible Study
lifeway.com/justopenthedoor

Book
justopenthedoor.com

A Study of Biblical Hospitality

Just Open the Door

BIBLE STUDY

7-SESSION

(in)courage author
JEN SCHMIDT

Just Open the Door

One Invitation Can Change a Generation